Unleashing God's Supernatural Power from the Third Heaven to Prosper in All Areas of Your Life

* The Third Heaven (have a real throne room experience)
* Living by the Holy Spirit with Your Finances (how to prosper God's way)
* Prophetic Prayers that Lead to Prosperity with Your Finances
* Get Close to the King (Jesus)
* Taking Your Faith to a New Level

Get Your Anointed CDs

* anointed praise music you can order (brings the atmosphere of heaven to earth)
* CDs to conquer the financial kingdom (an anointing for prosperity)

Unleashing God's Supernatural Power from the Third Heaven to Prosper in All Areas of Your Life

---

Pastor John Feagin

Library of Congress Control Number: 2009909649
ISBN: Hardcover 978-1-4415-8068-9
Softcover 978-1-4415-8067-2

This book was printed in the United States of America.

To order additional copies of this book, contact:
Xlibris Corporation
1-888-795-4274
www.Xlibris.com
Orders@Xlibris.com
66837

Contents

Part 1

“The Third Heaven”

Prophet John Feagin

My introduction to the third heaven began in the year 2002. In the year 2000, my journey into the kingdom of God started. I wrecked my automobile, a very nice Corvette. I lived for the world at this time and was serving the world. I did not realize this because my eyes were blinded. At approximately 3:00 am, I was driving home; and as I had been drinking, I was driving very fast. It had been raining, and I lost control of that car and hit a group of trees and two telephone poles. That car was cut in half, and I was crushed in this car. I died on impact, and the paramedics cut me out of the car and somehow revived me and got a pulse and rushed me to a nearby hospital. I had broken ribs, punctured lungs, a major head injury, my ankle shattered. I was on life support for two months in a coma. The many doctors did not give me any hope for living.

They said I was too messed up, and it was a matter of time before I would pass away. I had a praying grandmother, and many people prayed for me. I could hear the people in the room talking about me, and what I heard was not good. My mind was still alert, and I spoke to the Lord in my mind and said, “Lord, I guess I will see you in a minute.” The Lord spoke back to me and told me “no, not yet. I have much for you to do for me on this earth.”

I told the Lord that he had the wrong guy, that I had certainly not lived a life that was pleasing to him. The Lord told me that he had chosen me long before I was ever born and he knew what I would become and how important I would be in his kingdom. The Lord told me how he would be using me to pray for people and how people would be healed and delivered for bondage. At the time, I had been backslid and was living for myself and had not been to a church in over three years. The Lord said to me that I had much to learn about his kingdom. So I woke up in another state where there was a rehab hospital for people who were severely injured. All of the people I saw were badly injured; I had a trachea in my throat that which I have the scar to this day. I had to learn basic life skills again at age thirty-eight. I could not even talk very understandably at the time, had to learn how to drive all over again, and had to be recertified before I could be behind the wheel again. I was finally released from the hospital and had to move in with my parents to recover enough so I could live on my own.

Well, I recovered quickly, and soon enough I was living by myself. I had lost the job I had at the time of my accident; I lost the condominium, the Corvette, everything. I still had God and my faith and began reading the Bible a lot. I read God's promises and all the miracles that he had done in the past. I would pray for people, and God would seem to answer my prayers. The Lord kept dealing with me, telling me he still had much for me to learn. I would read the Bible; and one day in the mail, a book came to me about the Holy Spirit, and I became very interested in this Holy Spirit and read a passage about being baptized in the Holy Spirit.

I read where the Holy Spirit came like a rushing wind and filled the whole house and how men had been speaking in other tongues. About that time, I heard a rushing wind, and I thought that the weather was getting bad outside and a storm was coming. I thought that I needed to roll up my car windows. I got up and looked outside, and it was sunny and about ninety degrees outside. Then I sat back down to read more, and oil started dripping off my right hand, and I was trying to wipe it off. More oil dripped, and soon as I would wipe and wash my hands, it would start again. I had no idea at the time that it was a manifestation of the Holy Spirit.

A few days later, I just thought it was something related to the accident I had been through. I still had no idea what it meant; I had gotten what I had prayed and asked for. In 2 Corinthians, apostle Paul was caught up to the Third Heaven. It states that he could not tell whether it was in body or spirit. This is all done by the spirit. You can do this also. This is all about using your faith; if you think that you cannot feel anything or see anything, use your faith. Receive it by faith. You keep doing this, and I promise you glory will come upon you more and more with each visit. Then you will start closing your eyes and feeling and seeing this.

Now Let's Catch Up to the Third Heaven

I want you to visualize everything I am saying. First get in a quiet place and praise the Lord for what he has already done in your life and tell him that you are catching up to the Third Heaven to be with him, to be in his presence. It is best to do this late at night or very early in the morning so you will not be distracted. This requires total concentration and determination on your behalf. First say, "Father, in Jesus's name, I am coming to the Third Heaven where you live." Confess, "Father, in Jesus's name, help me." Visualize that your spirit is coming out of your body and you are going right through the roof of your house and you are high above your house and you are looking down on the roof of your house. Then you are traveling through the clouds and ascending higher, and you are now going through the atmosphere of the earth. You are now stepping out into space, and angels are coming all around you and setting up angelic shields of protection, impenetrable force fields. Chariots of fire are coming all around you with warrior angels and guardian angels with swords of light drawn to protect you.

You are now going through the universe, and you are passing all of the planets and stars; you come right out of the universe. Right ahead of you is the second heaven where Satan's generals live. The spiritual wickedness, I mean the big demons. Your angels and chariots of fire are encircled around you, and the spiritual wickedness cannot advance on you or harm you in any way. You are leaving them in your vapor trails as you swiftly go right through; and you are leaving them behind you, below you.

I will give you their names in a moment, because you will need these to effectively do your warfare from the Third Heaven, when you are seated with Christ, in Christ. Now you are coming right up into heaven. You visualize that you are seeing streets of gold, the crystal sea, and the majesty of heaven. It is so beautiful, it is so majestic.

Now your angels are leading you right to the throne room of God. Your king Jesus is standing at the throne room welcoming you inside. You bow down before him and praise him and worship the Lord. Tell him that you love and adore him and you are so blessed being one of his children. Confess, "Lord, forgive me where I fall short of your glory." Then your king will say that you are forgiven and will tell you to come inside and sit on the throne with him.

Remember there is room enough for all of us on that throne, it is a privilege; as his child, he gives you this right when you are going to do warfare against the spiritual wickedness and Satan himself. Visualize that you are sitting on the throne with him and his glory is coming all over you. The boldness that you will need is building up inside you to fight this spiritual wickedness. Your sword of the spirit is coming alive, his word. Now Jesus is pulling you into his spirit, and you are seated with Christ, in Christ in heavenly places. You are high above everything in the universe, and everything is below you.

Now visualize that your heavenly father is sitting on his throne. He is so majestic and great that you cannot begin to describe him. Now when your father in heaven looks at you, he sees his son Jesus. You can ask what you will, just make sure it is righteous and holy.

First let's do some warfare against the enemy and all of his demons in hell and his generals, his spiritual wickedness. *Now let me tell you their names and what they do and cause to happen in your life and with churches.* They are the ones who will come against you when you are in the Third Heaven! Don't worry, they are already coming against you and have been for most of your life, so understand what these spirits are and pull down these strongholds and watch your life get better. Take authority from the Third Heaven.

Confess, in the authority of Jesus's mighty name, "I take authority in Jesus's name over all the spiritual wickedness and Satan and every strongman Satan has assigned to my life."

Demons and Their Ranks

- Greek: *archas*, principalities, chief rulers or beings of the highest rank and order in Satan's kingdom. (Ephesians 12; Colossians 2:10 King James Version)
- Greek: *exousias*, authorities, those who derive their power from and execute the will of the chief rulers. (Ephesians 6:12; Colossians 2:10)

Python—a Pythian serpent or dragon inspiring idolatry. A spirit of infirmity that is like a big snake that will wrap around you and squeeze the life of God out of you and your money also. Soothsaying, crystal ball gazing, astrology, fortune-tellers, sorcery, tarot card readers, *Harry Potter* movies, new age movements. Works well with the Jezebel spirit, satanic music, false religions, horoscope readers, psychic readers and psychic activities, predicting the future, and giving false advice for monetary gains. Will try and squeeze God's word and life out of you. Will wrap around you and squeeze the very life out of you, will squeeze your finances out of you, whatever it can.

Leviathan—a spirit, a twisting serpent said to exist in the abyss of the ocean over fountains of water. *A spirit of pride*, deception, miscommunication; to have condescending attitudes toward others in the Body of Christ; wants you to lash out at others; an independent attitude, self-glory, a lot of self-confidence, critical and condemning attitudes and thoughts; a desire to control others, to boast over achievements; a desire for a reputation; to want a position of authority. Leviathan symbolizes the evil one energizing as his external enemy. Leviathan is the enemy without us, the world, the flesh, the devil.

Jezebel—a spirit of witchcraft, rebellion, fulfilling the desires of the flesh, often involved in sexual acts, using sex as a tool to gain access into people's lives, believes sex is a path to power and influence. Uses sex to get her way, and men fall prey to this daily. A real deceiver, has no respect for people in positions of authority. Has unrealistic expectation of others' lives, a real perfectionist, a "queen bee." Very domineering, very jealous of others when she is not getting the attention she thinks she deserves. She is a hard worker. Very attracted to people of power, uses self-pity to manipulate others. *A very seducing spirit, very dangerous.*

Behemoth—a spirit described as a monstrous animal, a hierarchy of demons, rules over the domain of gluttony and is said to be the butler and cupbearer of hell, described as Satan himself. It seems probable that behemoth represents the evil one acting in the animal and carnal elements of man's own constitution. Behemoth is the enemy within us.

It is important to know the names of these beasts and what they do to you and what they can cause to happen in your life. Know your enemies and what has been defeating you. Most people do not have any idea about this and wonder how the devil is still attacking them.

They communicate with the demons that are here on earth with *communication lines, supply lines, feeder lines.* They can cause all kinds of trouble in your life. But the good news is you from the Third Heaven can sever these lines of communication by loosing legions of angels to sever, destroy, and rip up all of these lines. They are underlined on the previous page. Do this, and now you are ready for warfare.

Let me give you an example of how I defeat this spiritual wickedness and Satan and all demons in hell. I say, first of all, I call these beasts by name and say, for instance, "Python, I plead the blood of Jesus against you. Spirit of Infirmity, in the authority of Jesus's holy name, I cancel all of your assignments against me, I take away every legal right you think you have on me, I close every door open to you, and command you in Jesus's name to loose your hold on my life, in the authority of Jesus's name, I confess this now."

"You are subject to everything I am ordering you to do because I am high above you in Christ." I say to this demon, "Obey me right now. Furthermore, anytime you think or say my name, I send confusion and delusion upon you. I render you deaf, dumb, and blind anytime you think or say my name, and the blood of Jesus will come upon you when you even think my name. In Jesus's holy name, I break you and strip you of what power you have."

Do this with all of these demons, and of course, by all means do this to Satan and all demons in hell. Satan's strongman assigned to your life and his subordinate demons that are under the strongman's control. Loose them from all assignments and cancel their assignments. Take away every legal hold and legal right that they think they have on you.

Once you have come against Satan and this spiritual wickedness and all demons in hell. Then pray your prayers from the Third Heaven and start calling things that should not be, as if they were. You will see a major difference in your life and the lives of those you pray for.

Then love your father in heaven and King Jesus Christ. Yeshua the Christ, Son of the Living God. Spend some time with God and tell him how much he means to you. Praise him and really love him. Say, "You are in control, God, and in charge, and nothing is over until you say it is over."

Then line up a scripture with your own prayer and speak it. His will for you is what you need to line up with his word for your need. You can stay in his presence as long as you wish.

Then when you realize that you have much to do and have to go. Say, "I will be back soon," then it is time to start your journey back to the earth. Visualize your guardian angels and warrior angels are encircling around you, and chariots of fire are coming around you. Your chariot is covered and dripping in the blood of Jesus. The Lord has placed a container that your chariots are pulling. It is enough of his blood to cover the second heaven as you pass through. Now you start your descent back toward the second heaven.

You are moving swiftly now and blowing through the second heaven and releasing the container of the blood of Jesus. It covers the second heaven, and the spiritual wickedness is dissolving and fleeing from you. Now you are coming back in the universe, and you are passing the stars and planets, and you see the earth coming up.

You enter the atmosphere and are passing through it and are coming down through the clouds, and you see the United States; you keep coming down and spot the state where you live, and as you get closer, you spot the roof of your house. Closer you come to it, and you come right through your roof, and your spirit returns back into your body. You say I am back and start praising the Lord for allowing you to catch up to the Third Heaven.

Say, "Lord, you know I will be back as soon as tomorrow because I have many needs and issues in my life. I see more clearly now what I can do from the Third Heaven." Speak to your Lord and tell him what a privilege it is to be seated with you. Just praise him and worship him. Pursue having a closer relationship with the one who paid the price for you on the cross at Calvary.

Practice doing this daily and every time you are seated with Christ; in Christ, some of his glory will be upon you every time and after a while you will be operating in his glory. The gifts he gives you will be multiplied, and very soon, God will be working through you to bless other people with healing they have been praying for. You will become a very important vessel for the kingdom of God.

This has certainly changed my prayer life and relationship with my father in heaven and his son, King Jesus. This book will change your life if you will practice this heavenly technique for becoming closer to God. I wish to see people get closer to God and defeat Satan and his spiritual wickedness that many are not aware of.

Let us all go to this level and become more victorious in life. Give Satan back some of what he has been giving you for most of your life. This is a real throne room experience; God will download more gifts into you every time you catch up to the Third Heaven, and a little more of God's glory will be on you with every visit. Let me ask you, have you ever come against Satan and rebuked him and run him off? Starting the very next day, you are under severe attacks for days. Well, it was the spiritual wickedness that got you. You did not have any idea what was happening. It makes you think, "I really got Satan mad, and he is attacking me harder than ever." Follow this guide and be free from this.

Be a useful asset for the kingdom of God. If you have never been to the Third Heaven, it will get closer to God, and you will develop a powerful prayer life. You will become a powerful weapon against the enemy and be able to help many others. That is my goal to equip the saints. Remember, "We are destroyed for lack of knowledge." The next part of this book is about living by the Holy Spirit with your finances. This will bless you greatly.

Prayer of Impartation

Abba, Father, I come to you in the mighty and matchless name of King Jesus, Yeshua the Christ, Son of the Living God. Father, I ask you to let me see what I can do to become closer to you and how I can defeat the enemy and his spiritual wickedness that has been holding me back form receiving my full blessings. Let me become a bold people, more confident. Let this year be an intense year of favor. Let me walk under an open heaven. Let me have this throne room experience, and to let every person that practices and is faithful master this.

I call an open heaven over their health, finances, and family life.

I pray this in the mighty name of Yeshua, King Jesus Christ, Son of the Living God. Amen, amen, and amen.

It is done in the mighty name of Jesus.

Part 2

Living by the Holy Spirit with Your Money and Becoming Extremely Prosperous

Conquer the Financial Kingdom
Bonus: Debt Cancellation God's Way
Prosperity and Success Scriptures
Prophetic Prayers

All Straight from the Bible

Showing you how to prosper God's way and
come out of financial bondage
How to have debt cancellation according to God's word

How to draw prosperity into your life:
You can become very wealthy
by following Bible-based principles

This will change your life if you will confess this every day, that means to speak it aloud. This anointing for prosperity will come upon you too.

Ask yourself this question:

What do you have to lose?

Look what you have to gain:
The kingdom of God's prosperity and wealth

Introduction

The most important thing to know about this is to read this out loud daily, confess it; and this anointing for prosperity will come upon you, but you have to press in and be hungry for this.

* This guide will show you what to do and what not to do to get prosperity into your life. You must speak this, not just read silently, confess this! If you desire prosperity, what have you got to lose? Nothing has worked so far, right? Let's stop living in mediocrity, just getting by.

Listen to a prophet that is all about increase, healing, and prosperity.

Your life will be changed forever, in a good way!

I get so tired of hearing people say how much they are in lack, You can speak a curse over your own life if you are not careful.

"He who guards his lips, preserves his life."

Be more careful what you speak over your own life. Never curse anybody or their business because you think it is not right. Judgment is not for you to decide (one of the hardest things I have learned).

Mark 11:23 says, "You will have whatsoever you saith." That means you will have what you say or speak. So be careful what you speak or say.

If you speak lack over your life, that is what you will have.

If you speak good things, prosperity is what you will have. This is so simple, is it not? So in other words, stop speaking curses over your own life.

God's Formula for Wealth

So what is God's formula for wealth? Let's go through some scriptures and find out what it says.

Deuteronomy 8:18 says, "Remember the Lord, for it is he that giveth thee the power to get wealth." That means we will give you wisdom and knowledge to make yourself prosperous and wealthy, says that it pleases the Lord to make you prosper. Do you have kids? Doesn't it please you to give and bless your children? Your daddy in heaven, who is perfect and who is unfailing in his love, desires for you to prosper. If you're not prospering, you have got to ask yourself, why? Is it my fault, or maybe I am not doing enough of what is right? "*Thus saith the Lord,* "Follow my commandments so that you may prosper in everything you do." The Lord says "follow my commandments"—don't murder, don't steal your neighbor's wife, don't be greedy for other people's things, don't lie, don't cheat, don't steal. Is that something you can handle? *You have got to be generous.* Let's see what the scriptures say. *Palms 37:25* says, "I have been young and am now old, yet have I not seen the righteous forsaken, nor his seed begging bread?" *Psalms 37:26* says, "He is ever merciful, and lendeth; and his seed is blessed." *Jeremiah 29:11*—more money, prosperity scriptures; *Deuteronomy 7:13*—"He will love thee, and bless thee, and multiply thee, he will also bless the fruit of thy womb, and the fruit of thy land, thy corn, and thy wine, and thine oil, the increase of thy kind, and the flocks of thy sheep, in the land which he swore unto thy fathers to give thee." *Psalms 23:1* states this: "The Lord is my shepherd, I shall not want!" Take this one to heart, say this when you are desiring something and are lacking. *James 1:17* says, "Every good gift and perfect gift is from above, and cometh down from the *Father of Lights*, with whom is no variable, neither shadow of turning." *Ecclesiastes 5:10* says this about you: "Every man also whom God hath given riches and wealth, and hath given him power to eat thereof, and to rejoice in his labour: this is the gift of God." *Proverbs 28:20* says, "A faithful man shall abound with blessings: but he that maketh haste to be rich shall not be innocent." Now *Proverbs 22:2* says, "Listen to this: The rich and poor meet together; the Lord is the maker of them all." *1 Timothy 6:7* states, "For we brought nothing into this world, and it is certain we can carry nothing out." There are more scriptures about wealth and prosperity than anything else in this precious book, because we are called to prosper.

Want to know what his will is for your life? *Thus saith the Lord* (3 John 2), "I wish above all things, that thou mayest prosper and be in good health, even as your soul prospers." What? You mean that he wants me to prosper and be in good health and my soul to prosper? Yes. Your father in heaven wants you to prosper in every way possible, not to be in financial bondage. Not to lack for anything at all. Remember you are a son or a daughter of the king of the universe. Don't you think the king wants the best for his children? Of course he does. Believe it and receive it. If you doubt, you will do without; if you believe, you will receive. It is that simple! Cannot make it any easier for you.

Do you know there are even more scriptures supporting wealth and money than there are those talking against it? So there are essentially ten steps associated with God's formula for wealth. Before I tell you this, I have to explain something else to you: *the number 1 thing holding you back from achieving success or becoming prosperous in life.* It is a small thing we are all able to do. We can all come up with this. Guess what it is. It is holding millions of people back and blocking your blessings.

This thing I am talking about is *an excuse (a well-planed lie is what an excuse is).* We can come up with so many excuses not to do something. Then we can all justify this excuse. We all are capable of this, and it holds us back so much. Let's break this, it is very important to you, please realize this. I am telling you the 100 percent truth to see you prosper in every way possible. You have got to make a choice, make a change. Get over excuses, have a desire to change your ways. There are three areas, three factors: (1) the basics of yourself—what makes you tick, what you do to earn money, and how you can improve. What has God put on your heart to do or to become in life? (2) improve on your people skills—how you relate to others and how you treat your fellow man; (3) personal development—improve on yourself, where you are weak, identify this area of your life and make a change. An excuse can hold back your blessings; a blessing might be coming by you, and all you have to do is grab it and go for it. But most people will believe what Satan whispers in their ear, planting that seed to make them come up with an excuse. That is how Satan works on you: he whispers things in your ears. Remember, he used to be an angel of light. He knows how to get to you, and he disguises himself very well. You need to stop complaining about your job, your life, your finances. God cannot promote you with grumbling and complaining.

* Weigh your ego against your goals and determine which weighs the most. Be teachable and drop your own ego, it will keep you in financial bondage. Humble yourself, or the Lord will humble you. I would rather humble myself. A spirit of unforgiveness will open doors of sickness and disease and block your own blessings and keep you in more bondage. If someone did you wrong ten years ago, and you still hold on to that, it will hinder you from succeeding and prospering in life. In other words, work on improving yourself every day! Be the best you can at everything you do.

Ten Steps to God's Formula for Wealth

1. *Don't love money more than you love your God.* If you are all consumed about money, if you worry about money, that means that money is an idol to you. If you worry about money, you worry about how you are going to pay your bills, you worry about how you are going to take care of the mortgage. Guess what? That is money being ahead of God.

   The Word of God tells us to take every thought captive to the obedience of Christ. In Matthew 6:25-34, it says, "Don't worry about what you will eat or what you will wear because your God in Heaven already knows what you will need." There is no need to worry when you have faith. So if you are worried about money, guess what? That's nothing but deception from the pit of hell.

   The enemy wants you to worry about finances, wants you think about money to drive you away from God, because he knows that if you actually follow him, if you actually honor him, if you actually love him, if you actually serve him, God will prosper you and make you great in the gates of the city. So you will be blessed going in, and you will be blessed coming out. He will bless those who bless you, and he will curse those who curse you. The enemy of your soul knows this. Why? Because he reads the Bible more than you do, it's the truth!
2. *Work with a spirit of excellence as unto him.* That's what it says in Colossians. It says, "Work with all your might unto him." Would you say that you need some work in that area? Probably. But if you work your business with all your might as unto him, he is your boss. And when it comes to the time for a promotion, it does not matter what a jerk of a boss you have ahead of you because God is over him or her. And guess what? He sees what you do. He sees your diligence. He sees the extra hours. He sees the motivation. He sees the heart that you're pouring into it. He sees and will bless the fruit of your hands. Don't worry about your boss. God will promote you right above him.

Look at Joseph in the Bible. His story is so powerful. Joseph is blessed by the father with a vision, and then thrown into a pit. He is then enslaved, brought to Egypt to be a slave in a governor's house who worships a foreign god, and the Word says, "God prospered him. He is accused because of an adulterous wife." "Ooh, Joseph, come here honey." She looked at the fine young man and said, "I've got to have some of that."

And Joseph ran. He eventually gets falsely accused of committing adultery and is put in prison. God exalted him from prison to become the head of the most powerful nation of that time.

So you have nothing to worry about. It doesn't matter what man or woman is above you. That means nothing because God will bless the fruit of your hands. That's if you are working it as onto whom? Him.

Know that the money that he is blessing you with is for a much bigger purpose than just your material things.

3. Does that mean that God wants to bless you with material things? Yes, he does. But he does not want the material things to own your life.
4. *You have to know that it's God's money.* It's not yours. It's God's money. It comes from him, and there's a much bigger purpose for that money. He wants to multiply that money, but when you get caught up in it, he will not bless you with more. Why? Because you are on a road to destruction. If you are on a road to destruction, he's not going to give you more so that you wind up destroying your life.
5. *Be generous.* Don't hoard. Don't be stingy. God wants to bless you with more, but he won't unless you are a giver. He loves a cheerful giver. You have to train your children early to give 10 percent back to God, because you don't want to deal with adult children that won't do what God's financial kingdom calls them to do. They have to give willingly and cheerfully

so God will trust them with more and learn this at an early age. Let me ask you this, will you help out a poor man in the streets, or will you walk by and think, "Get a job, man"? Or will you think, "He is going to buy some alcohol or drugs." How do you really know, or are you just making an excuse not to help him or not to have to give?

6. *Give into the right soil. (This is the most important one I have learned personally. Makes all the difference in the world.)*

When I first learned this, I got a headache. In the Bible, it talks about the parable of the sower. It talks about four different types of soil a farmer will sow. Listen and read this closely!

There is the rocky soil; if you sow on rocky soil, it says it will sprout quickly because it has no root system. But it says it gets scorched quickly by the sun. It sprouts quickly and dies quickly.

The second type discussed is the hard ground. With hard ground, the birds of the air will come and steal it away.

The third soil is the thorny soil. This type of soil gets roots. As it pops up, it is choked out by the worries of life. That's thorny, so it eventually withers and dies.

The fourth type is the fertile ground, and it is the only type of soil in which you want to plant your seed. The Bible says that on fertile ground, there is a return of thirty-, sixty-, a hundredfold. Some of us are planting in fertile soil. It says that whatever you plant, then you shall reap.

Have you noticed that your income has not increased? Maybe it stayed the same. You have to think where you are sowing your seed. You might ask, "How do I know where the fertile soil is?" You have to look at the fruit. If you want your money to return back to you a hundredfold, you have to sow it into fertile ground.

7. *You need to realize that there is a time of plenty and a time of famine.* There are reasons of famine and seasons of plenty. That is absolutely scriptural. Joseph did this when God blessed his nation for seven years with great abundance. Are you in a season of plenty? If you are, know that the season of plenty is not for you to eat all of your seeds.

   That season of plenty is for preparation so that you may still prosper when other people are failing all around you financially. So in the book of Genesis, we see clearly how God has designed it.

   If you are in a season of famine and you are prospering where you are planted and you can be trusted with what you have, you will gain more. That's how the financial kingdom works. If you are in that season of famine, you better take care of everything you have. Have a spirit of excellence unto and during this time. He will cause you to prosper when other people are failing financially.

   Remember what we learned earlier? The Bible says that if you forget him in the time of prosperity, poverty awaits you around the corner. So if you are in a prosperous situation right now, don't you dare forget who owns it and how he blessed you.

8. *You have to prosper where you are planted.* Do you have dreams and visions of where you want to go and what you want to do? Are there places that you would like to visit? Have you gotten frustrated because your dreams have not come to pass?

   Let me tell you that it is a plan of the enemy to get your focus on what you do not have, instead of focusing on making yourself prosper right where you are. This is how people do it. They have a dream. Well, when I have a big business, then oh, I am going to lavish my people, and I am going to really take good care of my customers. But these lazy, broke people, I cannot stand them, they are driving me crazy.

   Or I might hear, "Well, if my wife would act right, I could do a lot better. If my wife would act right, then I would treat her better. If my wife would stop nagging me, then I would buy her flowers once in a while." It does not work that way.

You have to prosper where you are planted, under the current circumstances that you are in. Joseph in the Bible had a gift to interpret dreams. He used that gift in a prison, and that's what got him promoted all the way to the top overnight—because he prospered where he was planted. Was serving in the prison what he was equipped to run a nation, the most powerful nation at that time?

9. *You need to ask big.* Come on. God is not a small god. It says that his arms are not short and his ears are not deaf. The Bible clearly says that no mind has conceived, no eye has seen, and no ear has heard what God has in store for those who love him. You need to think bigger than what you are thinking. You need to think wider and taller than what you are thinking. And you need to ask in the way of God's size, not your size. I am asking God for millions of lives all over the world. That is what I am asking for.

My personal prayer: "God, let me have the people that nobody else wants where I can affect millions of lives all over the world, and it will not stop there, but that they will go out, and they will affect millions upon millions of people's lives. That millions of homes will be made right, and they will come into right standing with you and principles that work." Also, part of step 9 is what you need to ask for help. The Bible says if you need wisdom to just ask for it. If there is something you do not know how to do, ask and he will give it to you.

10. You need to understand that it is okay to fail. It is okay to make mistakes. There are ups and downs. In the down time, don't fret, don't freak out, just know that you are fully taken care of, that he loves you. "No weapon forged against you shall prosper!" There will be rainy days. There are times you are going to make mistakes, and I want you to stand on this. *It is okay if you mess up.* It's okay. Why? Because God's word says that his grace far exceeds the heavens. That is huge. His grace is enormous.

The only understanding of grace that we have is grace that our friends or family show us, and that is pretty pathetic, wouldn't you say? A small amount of God's grace reaches the heavens. The Word says that grace is never ending, which means that we have the grace to fall right into his arms. That he will brush off your knees and put you back on your feet again. How awesome is that?

As I mentioned previously, in all of my sins, in all of my greed, God still blessed me financially. Why? Because he is looking for an obedient heart that will fall into his arms instead of depending on their own. How awesome is that?

I painted a picture of a financial kingdom. A kingdom that spreads far and wide, but the head of the kingdom is *GOD.*

Will you submit to him so that he may prosper, so that he may bless you? He desires for you to be in good health.

God wants to see his people get out of bondage, financial bondage. God does not have a desire for you to be in financial bondage at all. Are you tired of financial bondage? Do you want to be free from it? Then commit your ways unto him.

Do you know why you are in financial bondage? Now do not get mad at this statement: "Because you allow yourself to be!" Speak God's word about prosperity that I gave you and about success. His word never returns to him void. That means unanswered. When you speak his word about this, it obligates him to fulfill his word. This is the truth!

Pastor John's Prosperity Knowledge

Seven Steps That Will Take You to Poverty, Avoid These!
Information to Draw Prosperity to You and Get Poverty Away from You

Step 1. Being lazy and halfhearted. So lazy and working halfhearted unto yourself or your boss. Let me say this again: work halfheartedly, and it is a guarantee that poverty awaits you.

Step 2. Being a fool, drunkard, glutton, or a wasteful person, and you will become poor.

Step 3. Having pride during times of prosperity, forgetting God, this brings on poverty.

Step 4. Hiding your sins. There's a scripture in Proverbs that says, "He who hides sin has poverty waiting for him." Basically, if you attempt to hide your wrongdoing, you will realize poverty.

Step 5. Love money, and that will bring poverty. If you desire money more than you desire anything else—more than God, more than your kids, more than your wife—then guess what, poverty will show up at your doorsteps.

Step 6. Be selfish and stingy. This is an absolute formula for poverty. People that do not give will be impoverished.

Step 7. Be fearful and poverty will come upon you. In Matthew 25, it talks about the servant who said, "I was afraid, so I hid my talent"; and God called him wicked, and he cast him out with weeping and gnashing of teeth. The servant says, "I was afraid and hid my talent," which means he did nothing with what was given to him.

If you do nothing with what God has given to you, it will be taken away. This could be your business, maybe the job that you have, the family that you have, the responsibility that you have. If you do nothing with the talents, if you're called to sing and you're doing nothing with it, it will be taken away from you and given to someone else who already has, and you will be cast out.

I am including verses on prosperity and success. Confess them, speak them. Decree and declare each one in the authority of Jesus's name, say each time, "For it is written in the blood of the Lamb, the blood of Jesus."

If you want God's blessings to come and overtake you, bless a Jewish person. (Remember Jesus, your king, is Jewish.) We serve a Jewish god!

Genesis 12:3 says, "I will bless those who bless thee."

He is speaking originally of Israel. Pray for the peace of Jerusalem. Pray for God to protect Israel and for angelic protection, an angelic shield to be constructed. Loose angels of protection, guardian angels, warrior angels, archangels—Michael, Gabriel, Raphael—to have swords drawn and defeat all the enemies coming against Israel.

It is a commanded blessing of the Lord to bless those who bless Israel, and his word says, "I will bless those who bless thee."

I will include a page about prayers for Israel. When you pray, say, "Father in heaven, in Jesus's name I receive the blessings of Abraham, Isaac, and Jacob and Joseph coming upon me." *Do it every day. What have you got to lose? Look what you have to gain: *the prosperity blessings of the Creator, that's what!*

Remember, after you pray, then receive that prayer being answered. And coming to pass, most people never receive a prayer being answered.

Always receive the prayer that you just spoke being answered and coming to pass in your life.

Then watch this. Use your faith to draw that blessing to you. We have all been given the same measure of faith. Remember, "He is no respecter of persons." When you wake up the next morning after praying that night, say, "Father in heaven, in Jesus's name, I know you heard my prayer last night, and I know my answer is on the way. My breakthrough is coming, it is on the way. Thank you, Father, for this blessing coming to me." Every day thank him for this blessing coming to you. That is using faith. Thanking him for what you don't have and what you cannot see like you already have it. That's faith.

Thus saith the Lord, "It is impossible to please him without faith." No matter what you do or how righteous you are, without using your faith, you cannot really please him.

* Never be jealous of someone else's prosperity or wealth. If someone gets something new, be happy, rejoice with them.
* If you are jealous and envious of what someone else has been blessed with, poverty will surely be drawn to you.
* You have no idea what that person had to go through or had to sacrifice in order for that blessing to come. Remember, "Judge not, lest ye be judged, thus saith the Lord."

Scriptures to Draw Success into Your Life

Confess, speak each scripture boldly, out loud, daily
What have you got to lose? Look at what you have to gain, everything

After each scripture, say the following:

I decree this, I declare this, for it is written in the
blood of the Lamb, the blood of Jesus.

**In the house of the righteous is much treasure: but in the revenues of the wicked is trouble.*

—*Proverbs 15:6*

*By humility and the fear of the Lord are riches and honor and life.

—*Proverbs 22:4*

*And the Lord thy God will make thee plenteous in every work of thine hand, in the fruit of thy body, and in the fruit of thy cattle, and in the fruit of thy land, for good: for the Lord will again rejoice over thee for good, as he rejoiced over thy fathers.

—*Deuteronomy 30:9*

**Then shall he give the rain of thy seed, that thou shalt sow the ground withal; and bread of the increase of the earth, and it shall be fat and plenteous; in that day shall thy cattle feed in large pastures.*

—*Isaiah 30:23*

*Every man also to whom God hath given riches and wealth, and hath given him power to eat thereof, and to take his portion, and to rejoice in his labour; this is the gift of God.

—*Ecclesiastes 5:19*

*And also that every man should eat and drink. And enjoy the good of all his labour, it is a gift of God.

—*Ecclesiastes 3:13*

*Wealth and riches shall be in his house: and his righteousness endureth for ever.

—Psalms 112:3

*And the Lord shall make thee plenteous in goods, in the fruit of thy body and in the fruit of thy cattle, and in the fruit of thy ground, in the land which the Lord swore unto thy father to give thee.
The Lord shall open unto thee his good treasure, the heaven to give the rain unto thy land in his season, and to bless all the work of thine hand: and thou shalt lend unto many nations and thou shall not borrow.
And the Lord shall make thee the head, and not the tail, and thou be above only, and thou shall not beneath; if thou hearken unto the Commandments of the Lord thy God, which I command thee this day, to observe them and to do them.

—Deuteronomy 28:11-13

*According as his divine power hath given unto us all things that pertain unto life and Godliness, through the knowledge of him that hath called us to glory and virtue.

—2 Peter 1:3

*Riches and honor are with me; yea, than fine gold; durable riches and righteousness. My fruit is better than gold, yea, than fine gold, and my revenue than choice silver.

—Proverbs 8:18-19

*And I will send grass in thy fields for thy cattle, that thou mayest eat and be full.

Deuteronomy 11:15

*But grow in grace, and in the knowledge of our Lord and savior Jesus Christ. To him be glory both now and for ever. Amen

—2 Peter 3:18

*For thou shalt eat the labour of thine hands; happy shalt thou be, and it shall be well with thee.

—Psalms 128:2

*And they shall build houses, and inhabit them; and they shall plant vineyards, and eat the fruit of them. They shall not build, and another inhabit; they shall not plant, and another eat: for as the days of a tree are the days of my people, and mine elect shall long enjoy the work of their hands. They shall not labour in vain, nor bring forth for trouble; for they are the seed of the blessed of the Lord, and their offspring with them.

—Isaiah 65:21-23

Verses to Speak to Draw Prosperity into Your Life

Speak this every day. What have you got to lose? Look what you have to gain: the kingdom's prosperity!

Say, "Father, in the name of Jesus, I receive my daily bread, this day, and my daily prosperity. I speak these prosperity verses, your word over my life this day and every day!"

After each verse, say, "*I decree this, I declare this, for it is written by the blood of the Lamb, the blood of Jesus!*"

He will love Thee, and bless thee, and multiply thee, he will also bless the Fruit of thy Womb, and the fruit of thy land, thy corn, and thy wine, and thine oil, the increase of thy kind, and the flocks of thy sheep, in the land which he swore unto thy fathers to give thee.

—Deuteronomy 7:13

Remember the Lord, for it is he that giveth thee the power to get wealth.

—Deuteronomy 8:18

Thine, O Lord, is the greatness and the power, and the glory, and the Victory, and the Majesty: for all that is in the Heaven and in the earth is thine: Thine is the Kingdom, O Lord, and thou art exalted as head above all. Both riches and Honor come of thee, and thou reignest over all: and in thine hand it is power and might: and in thine hand it is to make great, and to give strength unto all.

—1 Chronicles 29:11-12

The Lord is my shepherd, I shall not want.

—Psalms 23:1

I have been young, and now am old, yet have I not seen the righteous forsaken or his seed begging bread. He is ever merciful, and lendeth: and his seed is blessed.

—Psalms 37:25-26

Yea, the Lord shall give thee that which is good, and our land shall yield her increase.

—Psalms 85:12

The righteous shall flourish like the palm tree: he shall grow like a cedar in Lebanon. Those that be planted in the house of the Lord shall flourish in the courts of our God. They shall bring forth fruit in old age: they shall be fat and flourishing: to show that the Lord is upright: he is my rock, and there is no uprighteousness in him.

—Psalms 92:12-15

Every man also to whom God hath given riches and wealth, and hath given him power to eat thereof, and to rejoice in his labour: this is the gift of God.

—Ecclesiastes 5:19

For I know the thoughts that I think toward you, saith the Lord, thoughts of peace, and not of evil, to give you an expected end.

—Jeremiah 29:11

He (God) has not left himself without witness, in that he did good, and gave us rain from heaven, and fruitful seasons filling our hearts with food and gladness.

—Acts 14:17

Every good gift and every perfect gift is from above, and cometh down from the Father of Lights, with whom is no variable, neither shadow of turning.

—James 1:17

He that spared not his own son, but delivered him up for us all, how shall he not with him also freely give us all things.
—Romans 8:32

Beloved I wish above all things that thou mayest prosper and be in good health, even as thy soul prospereth.
—3 John 2

It shall come to pass, if thou shalt hearken diligently unto the voice of the Lord thy God, to observe and to do all his Commandments which I command thee this day, that the Lord thy God will set thee on high above all nations of the earth: and all these blessing shall come on thee, and overtake thee, if thou shalt hearken unto the voice of the Lord thy God.
—Deuteronomy 28: 1-2

Keep the charge of the Lord thy God, to Walk in his ways, to keep his statues, and his commandments, and his judgments and testimonies, as it is written in the Law of Moses, that thou mayest prosper in all that thou doest, and whosesoever thou turnest thyself.
—1 Kings 2:3

They rose early in the morning, and went forth into the wilderness of Tekoa: and as they went out Jehoshaphat stood and said, "Hear me, O Judah, and you inhabitants of Jerusalem! Believe in the Lord your God, and you shall be established: believe and remain steadfast to his prophets, and you shall prosper."
—2 Chronicles 20:20

He (Uzziah) sought God in the days of Zechariah, who had understanding in the visions of God: and as long as he sought the Lord, God made him to prosper.
—2 Chronicles 26:5

Then shalt thou prosper, if thou takest heed to fulfil the statues and judgments which the Lord charged Moses with concerning Israel: be strong, and of good courage, dread not, nor be dismayed.

—1 Chronicles 22:13

In every work that he (Hezekiah) began in the service of the house of God, and in the Law, and in the Commandments to seek his God, inquiring of and yearning for him, he did with all his heart, and prospered.

—2 Chronicles 31:21

If they (the righteous) obey and serve him (God) they shall spend their days in prosperity, and their years in pleasures.

—Job 36:11

They shall prosper that love thee, peace be within thy walls, and prosperity within thy palaces.

—Psalms 122:6-7

Honour the Lord with thy substance, and with the First Fruits of all thine increase: So shall thy barns be filled with plenty, and thy press burst out with new wine.

—Proverbs 3:9-10

Confess these words over your life every day to gain financial prosperity; in his word, it says, "His word can return void." That means it will be answered if you speak it. It is up to you. Let's stop feeling sorry for ourselves and start confessing God's word, and you will see what happens.

Prophetic Prayers

Power Prayers that Will Change Your Life

Confess, speak these prayers daily and see the results. This will change your life.

The secret is to do this every day.

My Confession to My Father in Heaven and King Jesus to Prosper

Abba Father, in the name of your son, Jesus, I confess your word over my finances this day. As I do so, I say it with my mouth and believe it in my heart and know that your word will not return to you void, but will accomplish what you sent it to do. Therefore, I believe in the name of Jesus that all my needs are met, according to Philippians 4:19. I believe that because I have given tithes and offerings to further your cause, Father, gifts will be given to me; good measure, pressed down, shaken together, and running over will be poured into my bosom. For with the measure I deal out will be measured back to me.

Father, you have delivered me out of the power of darkness into the kingdom of your dear son, where I have taken my place as your child. I thank you that you assumed your place as my father and have made your home with me. You are taking care of me and even now are enabling me to walk in love, in wisdom, and in the fullness of fellowship with your son.

Father, I thank you that your ministering spirits are now free to minister for me and bring in the necessary finances, my harvest.

I confess that you are a very present help in times of trouble and that you are more than enough. You are able to make all grace (every favor and earthly blessings) come to me in abundance, so in all circumstances, I can give back into your kingdom and keep my blessings always flowing.

Sowing and reaping is my way. If I sow into good ground, I know that you will bless me and open new doors in my life. I do not hope this, I know this. Thank you, Father, my blessings are flowing to me in the mighty name of Jesus. I Thank you, I love you, I adore you. I bless you, Holy Father, I bless you, Holy Spirit, I bless you, King Jesus!

I confess this and pray this in Jesus's name. Amen, amen, and Amen.

End-of-Times Wealth Transference

Abba Father, I lose in heaven my supernatural
end-of-times wealth transference,

Hidden riches in dark places flowing into my life right
now in the mighty name of King Jesus

I am in agreement with the person reading this, and as
they speak it, it is done, it is finished, it is so.

In Mark 11:24, it states, "Therefore I say unto you, what
things soever ye desire, when ye pray

believe that ye receive them, and ye shall have them." I
believe that is flowing into my life

and I receive this coming to pass in my life.

All is a gift from you, Abba Father, in Jesus's name.

Thank you, Abba Father, in Jesus's name, for this prayer
being answered.

Prayer for a Year of More Than Enough: A Year of Reaping, a Year of Breakthroughs

Abba Father, Father God Almighty,

In the mighty name of Jesus, I proclaim and decree this new year 2009 to be abundant in every way. My health will be radiant, my finances will be more than enough, my family and my children will be blessed. I myself will be closer to you than ever before. Your warrior angels and guardian angels will be with me every step of the way. The fire of God and a double portion of your Holy Spirit and your glory will be guiding my every step. My angels of finances and prosperity will every day go ahead of me, before me, and prosperity in every way will flow to me. My soul will prosper the most, and I will be an asset to your kingdom. Flow through me hard this year of 2009.

I thank you for this abundant year, where there will be no lack. This is my year of more than enough, because you are the god of more than enough, My breakthroughs will come. Everything I have been praying for, you will manifest it in my life this year.

Now, Father, I know you have just heard me decree this prayer over my life, and I thank you for bring this prayer to fruition.

I bless you, Holy Father. I bless you, Holy Spirit. I bless you, King Jesus, my everything!

I pray this and all prayers in the mighty name of King Jesus. Amen, amen, and amen.

Jesus is the vine, and we are the branches; any branch that doesn't bear much fruit will be pruned so it will bear much fruit, but pruning has to take place.

Any branch that does not bear any fruit will be cut off.

Prayer of Petition

Father, in the mighty name of Jesus, I come to you now with this prayer of petition. I receive you answering this prayer as Mark 11:24 states that whatsoever I pray for, I believe I receive it, and I shall have it.

I humbly ask to give me a grant of the monies I need to sustain myself through this season, I ask you to loose these supernatural funds to me. I petition you, Father, to provide me with finances to sustain me, and I believe you hear this prayer from me, Father, and all things are possible to him that believe, and I believe.

This is my statement of my urgent, impossible needs. But with you, all things are possible, and I receive it in the matchless name of Jesus.

It is done, it is finished, it is so in Jesus's name.

Amen, amen, and amen.

Thus Saith the Lord of Hosts Prosperity Scriptures

They shall not be ashamed in the evil time: and in the days of famine, they shall be satisfied.

—Psalms 37:19

Thou comest the year with thy goodness; and thy paths drop fatness.

—Psalms 65:11

Thou has caused men to ride over our heads; we went through fire and through water: and thou broughtest us out into a wealthy place.

—Psalms 66:12

And Abraham was very rich in cattle, in silver, and in gold.

—Genesis 13:2

And I will make of thee a great nation, and I will bless thee, and make thy name great; and thou shall be a blessing.

—Genesis 12:2

Recall the story of Joseph:

And all the countries came to Egypt to Joseph to buy corn; because the famine was so sore in the land.

—Genesis 41:57

Prayer for a Season of Intense Favor

Abba Father,

Yahweh Almighty, in Yeshua's mighty name, I call heaven and earth to record, I declare this decree before heaven and earth right now.

I thank you. Father, in the mighty name of Jesus, I proclaim and decree and declare that this is a season of intense favor of the Lord Jesus Christ upon my life. A season of intense financial favor. I pray that you will take every ounce of weariness out of my physical, emotional, mental, and spiritual state. I pray that you will bring me to a place of laughter, love, and fresh intimacy in the matchless name of Jesus. Father, I pray that I will come to such a place of joy and delight, that I will be transformed into a different person.

I ask, Lord, that your intentionality in this matter will be transmitted into my heart fully day after day after day. You will teach me how to rest, how to worship. That I will have a season of learning how to live in that fragrant presence of God. I ask that all you want to say to me, and be to me, will come to me without hindrance or lack. That you will come down into my heart with your goodness and transform me. Transform my thinking, my praying, and my very being before you.

That I will become a forerunner of a bold and intimate people who are confident in the very nature of God. That I will become a pioneer of a new way of praying in the spirit.

That, Father, you will teach me to come before you like a much loved bride. That I would pray with joy and delight and laughter. That, Lord, my yoke will be easy, my burden will be light, because I have learned how to love the king in a deeper way.

I pray this in King Jesus's mighty name.

Close by Thanking God

* I thank you, Lord, that you have heard my prayer and that every curse over my life has been revoked and canceled.
* I thank you, Lord, that I have been delivered from the domain of darkness and translated into the kingdom of your love.
* I thank you, Lord, that Satan has no more claims against me or my family or anything else that you have committed unto me.
* I thank you, Lord, that from now on, as I walk in obedience, your blessings will come upon me and overtake me.

Now, believe that you have received; this will open you up to all the blessings God has for you!

Confession When You Plant Your Seed or Tithe

Abba Father, in Jesus's name, I plant my seed, I release my seed in good fertile ground, good soil, fertile soil. I receive my harvest from you. Lord, of the harvest, this is what I am believing my seed to produce in my life.

Father, in Jesus's name, I am believing you for supernatural monies to come from the north, south, east, and west to come forth in my life more work, raises, bonuses; for unexpected checks to come in the mail, for supernatural monies to show up in my bank account, I am believing you for debt cancellation, for divine wisdom and knowledge, uncommon favor with the seed I have just released to happen in my life this coming week. Lord of the harvest, I am trusting you and releasing my faith. For in your word you say that without faith, it is impossible to please you, and I am using nothing but faith *and faith alone*. Lord of the harvest, I trust in you. For you are Jehovah Jireh, the Lord my provider, and you shall supply all of my needs. The same measure I deal out shall be measured back to me, and I receive it coming to pass in my life.

Abba Father, Father of lights, I give with expectancy, and I know that you will water my seed, and it shall grow into a mighty harvest and produce what I am believing for. I do not hope, I know my blessings are coming.

In your word, it states, "Give and it shall be given unto you, pressed down, shaken together, and running over" and I receive this coming to pass in my life.
"You shall cause men to give back into my bosom." (Say this statement three times.) *"I shall not lack any good thing."*
Every curse is broken and reversed, and every blessing is loosed and released upon my life right now.
Thank you, Father of lights, for the wonderful blessings coming this week into my life.

It is done, it is finished, it is so
in the mighty name of King Jesus. Yeshua the Christ, Son of the only Living God! Thank you, Lord, for this harvest coming into my life. I give you all the glory and will tell people what you have done for me through this coming harvest and will glorify your name.

Yahweh Almighty, if it pleases you, please honor your word about sowing and reaping, because I, ______________, I release my faith, I receive my blessings from you, Father of lights, in Jesus's mighty name.

Father, in Jesus's name, I call heaven and earth to record right now, I declare this decree that you, Jehovah Jireh, the Lord my provider, will send someone into my life capable of promoting me and blessing me.

Father, in King Jesus's name, I thank you and praise you
for these blessings coming into my life.
Father, I know some major blessings are coming into my life,
and I receive them in Jesus's matchless name.
Yeshua the Christ, Son of the only Living God, I pray and
confess this with faith and faith alone.
I know it is done and finished, and I receive this decree coming
to pass in my life right now.
Now I say,
amen, amen, amen.

The Prayer of Release from All Curses

Lord Jesus Christ, I believe that you are the Son of God and the only way to God and that you died on the cross for my sins and rose again from the dead.

I give up all my rebellion and all my sins, and I submit myself to you as Lord, I turn to you, Lord Jesus, for mercy. From now, I want to live for you. I want to hear your voice and do what you tell me.

I confess all my sins before you and ask for your forgiveness. I especially ask for forgiveness for any sin that was exposed as a curse, whether committed by me or my ancestors or others related to me. (Add personal details of this.)

By a decision of my will, I forgive all those who have harmed me or wronged me, just as I want God to forgive me; in particular, I forgive (add names that relate to this).

I renounce all contact with anything occult or satanic or any secret society that binds me against the will of my father God. I commit myself to remove any objects linked to these forbidden areas or activities. I cancel Satan's claims against me.

Lord Jesus, I believe that on the cross, you took upon yourself every curse that could ever come against me, so I now release myself from every curse, every evil influence, and every dark shadow over me or my family, from any source whatsoever, in your name, King Jesus.

By faith, I receive my release and thank you for it.

Amen, amen, and amen!

Prayer to Turn Around from Negative Words and Curses Spoken from Others

Father God Almighty, in the mighty, mighty name above all, the matchless name of Jesus,

I come before your wonderful throne of grace, I humble myself before you.

I enter your gates with thanksgiving, your courts with praise, and I bless the name of Jesus, my Lord, my savior, my king. Father, many people are jealous of me and speak negative words and curses over my life, because they do not want me to prosper or succeed in my endeavors. They want me to fail.

This will not happen, because I have authority of this world, because of Jesus my king that was crucified on that cross at Calvary and gave me authority over this world. Father, I use my authority right now.

Father, in Jesus's name, I call heaven and earth to record, I declare this decree!

All negative words and curses spoken over my life by anyone human or demon that is meant to harm me or destroy my life.

Every time someone speaks a curse over my life, you, Yahweh Almighty, in Jesus's name, will cause me to prosper and succeed, and I shall be blessed more with every negative word and curse.

What the devil meant to harm me, you will use to prosper me and bless me.

Every curse is reversed, and many blessings are loosed upon my life from this day forward.

Part 3

Debt Cancellation, God's Way

This section of this book is right next to prospering God's way. It deals with debt cancellation God's way. If God can prosper you, he can cancel debts that are against you as well. We have to realize that God, the creator of the universe, can do anything he desires. This section gives you the formula to have debt cancellation. I also give you the laws for debt cancellation.

The one thing you have to realize is that it takes faith to achieve this, and believe God for this. God can cause money to manifest in your bank account or in the account of whatever debt you owe. If you follow my formula for this, you can have this as well. Start confessing, thanking God for this coming to pass in your life. Open your mouth and start using the power of the tongue; remember life and death are in the power of the tongue.

Let us think about this statement if we were riding down the road and we passed a nice Mercedes on the side of the road. The price tag looked very expensive, around $50,000, and the automobile itself looks very appealing, and the paint job is flawless. This car is not but one year old. One of the first things out of your mouth is "how beautiful the car is, but I surely cannot afford that car." Well, guess what, you just spoke that you can't afford it, and because you spoke it over your life, you never will. That statement came out of your mouth for your life. You should have said, "I do not have the money for that at this time, but the Lord is fixing to bless me with more than that, and I am going to buy a new one."

The power of your own tongue can make you or break you. Debt cancellation is one of the unlimited blessings the Lord can bring into your life. Read and study this and allow it to absorb into your spirit. I have watched many people achieve this and have spoken this into the lives of people, and it happens. All I tell people is to just have faith and trust God to make this happen in their life and have no doubts. If you have doubts, it will cancel your blessing. God cannot work with any doubts at all.

I know this book sounds incredible, and the things I have written are things you need in your own life. Have you ever read the scripture "If you have faith as a grain of mustard seed, nothing shall be impossible unto you"?

Well, I am fixing to give you the steps to take to walk in this, followed by the laws of debt cancellation. Then there will be a prayer to confess over your own life to have this. I desire to see people receive this and believe that God can do this, and to build up their faith in God.

Let me be clear with this. You may say that "he is a prophet, a pastor, that is why he can do this." That has no bearing on this at all. God is no respecter of persons; and what he does for one, we will do for another. It is all about your faith level and how much you can believe God to bring it to pass in your life. Do not believe that you can go out and buy things and get in debt on purpose and God will cancel your debts, because you have to be a good steward with your money. You have got to be wise with your money and handle spending it with wisdom and not overloading yourself with bills. Use your head and do not buy things just because you want it; sure, material things look good, and television commercials and sales papers make things look real good. If you are just barely making it, you do not need to create bills. Be happy and content with what you already have and be thankful that God has provided you with this that you already have. It may not be new, but it is paid for and all yours. Now let me take you through the steps.

Step 1. Develop a clear understanding that God desires for you to live an abundant life here on earth (John 10:10), and then make a quality decision to get out and stay out of debt.

Step 2. Build your faith and confidence in God by diligently studying what his word has to say concerning debt cancellation.

Step 3. Gather all your bills together in one place. On a sheet of paper, write your declaration of independence from debt and place it with your bills.

Step 4. Confess aloud how much you owe to whom as well as your scriptures on debt cancellation. Do this several times daily until you see results.

Step 5. Bind the strongman (debt) assigned to you and loose him from his assignment. Loose angels of God to bring forth your harvest.

Step 6. Tithe faithfully into a Word-based church and obey God in your giving. Be sure to be a cheerful giver.

Step 7. Sow into the life of an anointed vessel of God. Become a partner with the anointing that is on their life. Sow into them and their ministry, and reap the anointing on their life.

Step 8. Maintain high levels of joy, prayer, and praise for God for your release from debt. Begin thanking God now for the manifestation of debt release, and remember to give him glory for every victory, no matter how small it may be.

Step 9. Guard your heart and refuse the temptation to speak anything negative against your financial situation. Be careful what you speak; in the book of Mark, it says, "You will have whatsoever you saith." Also be careful of how you think; "as a man thinks, so is he."

Step 10. Do not ever reject God's instruction on doing or giving to someone, no matter how strange it may seem to you. Obedience brings provision. Obedience is the key. Remember one word from God is all it takes to change your life forever!

Step 11. Always keep the mission for wealth at the forefront of your thinking. (Genesis 12:3)

If you will follow these steps and not grumble and complain, it shall come to pass, and you will become free of debt. This is God's plan to bring about debt cancellation and become debt free. You will become the lender and not the borrower.

Revelation knowledge from prophet John Feagin www.anointedman.com

Next, a debt-cancellation affirmation prayer, confess this daily, make up your mind that you will not stop until God blesses you. I will give you the laws of debt cancellation, follow these Bible-based principles. The key is to confess these words daily and receive this coming to pass in your life. Do this from the Third Heaven, seated with Christ in heavenly places.

Laws of Debt Cancellation

Text: Romans 13:8

I am going to challenge you today to rise in the authority of the believer today. I want to talk to all of us about taking advantage of what the Spirit has made available unto us.

Read text

The Amplified Version of this scripture says, "Keep out of debt and owe no man anything accept to love one another. For he who loves his neighbor, who practices loving others, has fulfilled the law, relating to one another's fellow men. Meeting all of its requirements."

I thought it was very interesting that in the same scripture, at the same time, he talks bout owing no man anything (being debt free). He talks about the importance of loving every man. You see, we cannot expect for supernatural power to be released in the lives of someone who lives outside of the circle of love. It is not just talking about certain principles to get you out of debt. I am talking about supernatural debt release.

In order for supernatural debt cancellation to happen in our lives, we have to make sure the door of our heart is open and that there is nothing hindering God's supernatural power. And in this passage, God wants us to see how important it is to walk in love when we are believing God to owe no man nothing. It is very difficult for God to do a miracle in our life when we walk in unforgiveness with another person, when we have fought against someone, when we walk in jealousy and envy against a person, when we have bitterness against a person.

So scripture tells us, "Owe no man nothing, but to love him." Walking in true love with others is the key that releases God to show up in our life to be able to have magnificent things. Don't expect God to be able to come and give you a miracle of healing, or financial increase, when you don't walk in *true* agape love. God wants us to understand how important it is to maintain the right kind of character so he can move in our lives.

A lot of people want to act like a fool and try to be cool and expect the power of God to flow through their life. But it won't work. The power of God cannot move in someone's life who is not living holy and living according to God's word. If we will live a holy life and walk in the love of God, there are a lot of things that will be taken care of in our life.

We are talking about the laws that will release supernatural debt cancellation. But before we get into that, let's talk about why debt is such a problem.

Five reasons why it is such a problem (besides that fact that 95 percent of the people sitting in churches this morning are in debt):

1. Debt promotes discontentment.
   When we charge things with money we don't have, we will not be content with our income. We are not going to be patient. When a person acquires things too easily without the pride of ownership, it is easy to become dissatisfied easily.
2. Debt makes arrogant presumptions about the future.
   People assume that down the line, they will have the money to handle the debt they just charged. Without knowing exactly what the future holds. This is presumptuous.
3. Debt requires you to transfer your future wealth to your creditors.
   Wealth that could be yours, wealth that you could be saving and investing is transferred to the creditors.
4. Debt limits your options.
   Not only will it limit your options. But heavy loads of debt will eliminate them altogether. You don't have the right to choose what you're going to do because of the debt.
5. Debt steals your freedom and makes you a slave.
   When we are under a load of stupid debt, we are in bondage. We have no way out but to work off our sentence. And King Solomon, the wisest man to ever lived, summed it up this

way (Proverbs 22:7), "The rich rule over the poor, and the borrower is servant to the lender."

There are principles for obtaining debt cancellation. I believe the believer has an anointing advantage. This simply means there is authority that has been given to the believer. That if we use that authority properly, we can see God showing up and doing supernatural things. The only way this is going to happen is to have some believers in the house. In these times and days, believers just don't believe God like they used to. I mean the church used to believe that there was nothing impossible for God. Now we see people having more confidence in their intelligence than we do the supernatural power of God. I don't know about you, I just trust the power of God. I believe these books from Genesis to Revelation—I believe it!

I am not a debater, I am a believer. My question to you today is, do I have any believers in this house? Because what I am getting ready to teach us today is going to go past the intelligence of our mind-set. It is going to require plain, old-fashioned believing and receiving. We need to make the choice today to believe God, believe his word, and set our life for the supernatural power of God to show up. And allow him to do things that we didn't think he could do. I am telling you that what I am about to teach you won't make sense to your natural mind, but it will make faith.

I am about to lay out a war plan against debt. I am going to give us a supernatural war plan against debt. I believe God is about to do something extraordinary in our lives. I believe God is about to do something supernatural today. I believe God is about to do something that we can't even figure out, and all we will be able to do is go home and say, "That's God." It won't be able to explain to itself. But I need some people that are going to believe. Some people that will receive.

Let's look at this battle plan against the spirit of debt.

Step 1. Walk in agape love with everyone.
Romans 13:8

Step 2. Decree daily debt free
Luke 4:18

Notice he has called us to preach the gospel to the poor (or those without). I have an announcement to make: "I have been anointed to preach this gospel to you today." Notice he says we are to proclaim liberty to the captives. If you are in debt, you are captive.

The Amplified Version says, "The Spirit of the Lord is upon me, because He has sent me to preach the good news, the gospel to the poor. He has sent me to announce release to the captives." TO ANNOUNCE RELEASE TO THE CAPTIVES.

I believe first things first. I have a message for you today, and it is this: SOMETHING IS ABOUT TO BE RELEASED OVER YOUR HOUSE. I announce to all of ROC, you are released from debt. I have just announced your deliverance and your release from the spirit of debt.

There is a demonic force trying to keep us bound in debt, and I have just taken authority. I have just made a decree; and the book of Job says, "If you decree a thing, then I will bring it to place." See, some of us are not seeing things happen because we haven't said anything. We haven't decreed anything. But when I made that announcement a few moments ago, you were not the only one to hear it. Heaven heard it, angels heard that announcement, demons heard that announcement. I ANNOUNCE THAT YOU ARE RELEASED FROM THE SPIRIT OF DEBT!

And the Bible says that angels harken after the Word of God that comes out of our mouth. Demons are paralyzed by the Word that comes out of our mouth. WE ARE RELEASED. According to scripture, only after a thing has been decreed can we walk in it.

A man that has been given twenty years for murder can't walk out unless the governor decrees it. I just announced your release, but I said I need some believers in the house. So if I just announced your release, I need you to tell me what it is. Tell someone, "I am released, I am free from debt." I am talking supernatural right now. I am talking about something that cannot be explained. I am talking something supernatural.

The devil doesn't want that announcement to be made. You must understand nothing starts without a decree. This church *is* debt free. IS THERE ANYTHING TOO HARD FOR GOD!

Step 3. Bind the spirit of debt
Matthew 12:28-29

We have been given spiritual authority. We use it for sickness and depression, but why not debt? We think this is just about spending. And we need to do what is right in the natural. We can't spend more than we earn. But we must understand the supernatural to this. I want to spoil the devil's house, but I can't do it till I first bind the strongman.

How can we stop debt from flowing in our lives when the spirit that is behind debt is still allowed to work? Here is the problem. Nobody ever thinks about the fact that this could be a demon spirit behind this. Satan came in the Garden of Eden slick. The only thing he did was make a suggestion to Eve. A suggestion to something that seemed pleasing to her natural man.

The most powerful weapon of the enemy is the power of suggestion. There is a demon spirit behind debt. For example, you already have $100,000 worth of debt. And you go into a store and see something you want, and you hear a suggestion, "Why don't you use credit? After all, it is interest free for five years." See, many already can't obey God because of debt.

The plan of the enemy is to get everyone in the Body of Christ in debt. So when the time comes to do for the kingdom of God what needs to be financially done, they won't be able to do it because they took all of the suggestions of the enemy. The enemy wants to build a wall of containment to keep us in one place. And every time we get increased, the enemy is right there to show us something to blow it on. The more we make, the more we spend.

The enemy wants us to be in hyperconsumption mode. So if we get a raise, it won't matter. See, people are trying to get out of debt without binding the strongman. If you are going to spoil his house, someone has to tie him down.

So if I go to the mall, knowing I am working on getting out of debt, if I have bound the strongman, I can walk out without using credit, because I got him bound. But as long as he is able to make suggestions and manipulate.

See, much of the Body of Christ today does not really believe in demons. If we could see in the spirit realm. And because of this disbelief, people never get to the root of the matter. Because their religion has taught them that these spiritual things don't exist. These people will believe in angels, but not demons.

The Bible says in Ephesians 6, "We wrestle not against flesh and blood, but against principalities, and authorities and rulers of the darkness and wickedness in heavenly places." THESE ARE DIFFERENT CLASSES OF DEMONS. They are sent to suggest and possess.

Believers cannot be possessed, but can be oppressed. If your thinking is not lined up with the Word. If someone makes you mad, and you cuss them out, you are fighting the wrong way. All that leads to is them cussing you out, and you'll keep going back and forth; but if you want to get to the root of it, go to your prayer room and declare the Word against that spirit behind them. BIND THAT SPIRIT, and declare that spirit has no authority.

THINGS CAN CHANGE WHEN YOU REALIZE WHAT YOU ARE FIGHTING.

The devil didn't make Adam and Eve eat the fruit in the garden. He just made the suggestion. He doesn't make us cuss someone out, he just makes the suggestion. He doesn't make us do what violates God's word, he only makes the suggestion. He is not that powerful; HE CAN'T MAKE US DO ANYTHING WE DON'T WANT TO DO. He can suggest it, but that doesn't mean we have to do it.

The credit card in our wallet or our purse can become a tool of suggestion.

It takes money to spread the gospel, and most of what we could be using to promote the gospel to the nations is being sent to the world's creditors every month. If every person here were debt free, and they took simply their mortgage amount, that they budgeted anyways. If only they took that and gave it to the kingdom of God.

The world is spending billions to manipulate our children into their system. And we can't even raise enough money to start Christian educational systems. The world owns TV stations that charge ten million dollars for a one-minute spot during the Super Bowl. And the church cannot even afford to get on the local station to preach the gospel.

How long must we continue to be the seed of debt? How long must we serve the spirit behind debt?

Repeat after me: "In the name of Jesus, you demon force behind debt, you spirit of debt. In the name of Jesus, I bind you. And whatsoever I bind on earth is bound in heaven. I declare now that the spirit behind debt has been bound in Jesus's name."

Step 4. Get *intense* in the Spirit.
Matthew 11:12

Applying violent faith. IT IS TIME TO STOP ACTING LIKE A BUNCH OF SPIRITUAL SISSIES. It is time to get violent. Let me explain what that means. The literal translation of the scripture is, "Like a mighty army storming the gates of a city."

The Amplified Version of this passage says, "From the days of John the Baptist until present time, the kingdom of heaven has suffered violent assault, and violent men seize it by force, as a precious prize. A share in the heavenly kingdom is sought with most ardent zeal and intense excursion."

Intense—when something is intense. it is the intensity of the force that will take the victory.

We think that when the enemy attacks our body, that reading one scripture once per day is going to be enough. We think that in these last days, coming to church once a week will be enough. But the reality is the enemy is working every minute to destroy us.

See, most Christians are defeated not because the Word doesn't work, but because they don't know how to exert the Word of God in faith with intensity. These are violent times that require violent measures. THIS IS WAR!

The more intense you are, the quicker the results.

You can't sow an offering every once in awhile and expect to be debt free. You have to operate in biblical obedience. *Tithe* and *offering*. Read Malachi 3.

The Word needs to be worked with intensity. Declare debt free every day. Sow financial seed toward being debt free.

Declare every day you are walking in Abraham's blessings.

WE SPEAK TO THE MOUNTAINS OF LIFE.

Be prepared the devil will be right there to discourage you from being violent. But when he tries to tell you it isn't working, GET MORE INTENSE!

So from this point on, we are violent.

REAL FREEDOM FROM ANYTHING REQUIRES VIOLENCE.

We want the promise without the process.

But it is time to be violent.

Debt-Cancellation Affirmation Prayer

By Prophet John Feagin

God's word states that God delights in the prosperity of your servants. Therefore, as your servant, I declare that I am out of debt, and all my needs are met, and I have plenty to put in store.

> Let them shout for joy, and be glad, that favour my righteous cause: yea, let them sat continually, let the Lord be magnified, which hath pleasure in the prosperity of his servant. (Psalms 35:27 KJV)

I no longer operate by the world's system of debt cancellation, but by God's system of seedtime and harvest. I believe when I sow into good ground, I will reap a multiplied return, even up to and exceeding a hundredfold.

> Be not deceived; God is not mocked; for whatever a man soweth, that shall he also reap. (Galatians 6-7 KJV)

> And let us not be weary in well doing: for in due season we shall reap, if we faint not. (Galatians 6-9 KJV)

> And other fell on good ground, and did yield fruit that sprang up and increased; and brought forth, some thirty and some sixty and some an hundred. (Mark 4:8)

Be a cheerful giver, and sow under the direction of the Holy Spirit.

> Every man according as he purposed in his heart, so let him give; not grudgingly, or of necessity: for God loveth a cheerful giver. (2 Corinthians 9:7)

Have a hearing heart and meditate on God's word daily. As a result, you can hear God's voice clearly and operate in his wisdom and anointing.

> And thine ears shall hear a word behind thee, saying, this is the way, walk ye in it, when ye turn to the right hand, and when ye turn to the left. (Isaiah 30:21 KJV)

The Word states that "out of the heart, flow the issues of life." Therefore, refuse to allow anything to come before my eyes, in my ears, or out of my mouth that does not line up with the Word of God. I purpose to guard my heart diligently by bringing forth every thought, action, or desire into submission to the Word of God.

> Keep thy heart with all diligence; for out of it are the issues of life. (Proverbs 4:23)

As your word directs, I cast down thoughts of this world that run against the Word of God. I disallow the thoughts and processes of the world's method of debt and finance and look to you and your word.

> Casting down imaginations, and every thing that exalteth itself against the knowledge of God, and brining into captivity every thought to the obedience of Christ. (2 Corinthians 10:5 KJV)

As I continue to speak of debt-canceling scriptures over my finances, by the profession of my faith in God's word, to do that which it was set out to do, I acknowledge the legions of angels that have been dispatched on my behalf. I prepare and receive cancellation of my debts and full increase in my life; in Jesus's mighty name, I decree and declare I am released and loosed from my debts in the authority of Jesus's most holy name.

> Bless the Lord, ye his Angels, that excel in strength, that do his commandments, hearkening unto the voice of his word. (Psalms 103:20 KJV)

This I pray, all for the glory of God and furtherance of your work in my life; as your hand and favor rest upon my life, I commit to walking under the leadership of the Holy Spirit and fulfilling my role in the fields during this time of great harvest.

The Laws of Debt Cancellation

Prophetic Wisdom and Knowledge

Pray for the Peace of Jerusalem

I will bless those who bless thee, I will curse those who curse thee.
—Genesis 12:3

Be a blessing to Israel! God's blessings will come and overtake you.

Confess, "I call heaven and earth to record right now, I declare this decree."

* I pray Israel will be delivered form the murderous plans of her enemies. (Psalms 18:3)
* I pray Israel will be able to maintain constant vigilance. (Isaiah 62:6)
* I ask God to silence threats and false accusations of those who seek to destroy Israel. (1 Samuel 2:9)
* I pray Israel will be kept safe from terror attacks. (Psalms 91:5)
* Now say, "I loose, I loose, I loose hundreds and hundreds of millions of legions of angels to surround Israel with angelic hedges of protection, to set up impenetrable force fields, impregnable force fields and shields to protect Israel from her enemies. I call every hurting Israel citizen healed by King Jesus's stripes."
* Next, "I loose, I loose, I loose hundreds and hundreds of millions of legions of angels of prosperity, of provision, of finances to gather Israel money from the north, south, east, and west from all four corners of the earth and bring Israel *prosperity now, favor now, abundance now, provision now.* I speak this in the authority of Jesus's mighty name."
* I call that the enemies of Israel shall become their footstools.

Do this and you will be blessed; also do this for widows and orphans of the whole world.

Daily Prayers

(Pray Out Loud)

Heavenly Father, I (we) come to You now in the Name of my (our) Lord and Savior Christ Jesus. (Note—if two or more praying: Heavenly Father, _____ and I come to You in one accord in the Name of Christ Jesus of Nazareth according to Matthew 18:19). Holy Spirit, I (we) pray that You will quicken me (us) to hear my (our) Heavenly Father's Voice and lead me (us) in prayer. Holy Spirit, I (we) ask you to reveal to me (us) any un-confessed sins I (we) have in my (our) heart at any time. Heavenly Father, I (we) bow and worship before You. I (we) come to You with praise and with thanksgiving. I (we) come to You in humility, in fear, and in trembling and seeking truth. I (we) come to You in gratitude, in love, and through the precious Blood of Your Son Jesus Christ of Nazareth. Amen.

Forgiveness of Sin Prayer

Heavenly Father, I (we) come to You now in the Name of my (our) Lord and Savior Christ Jesus, I (we) make a joyful shout to You, we come before Your Presence with singing, and we enter into Your gates with thanksgiving, and into Your courts with praise. Lord through out this prayer and through out this day I pray for myself (ourselves) and the following people _____, _____, _____, and _____. Heavenly Father have mercy on me/us, our children and grandchildren, our friends and family and the people we have prayed for and according to Your loving kindness, and according to the multitude of Your tender mercies blot out all our transgressions, and wash us totally from our iniquities and cleanse us from our sins. For we do acknowledge our transgressions and our sin is always before us, and against You and You only have we sinned and have done this evil in Your sight. That You may be found just when You speak and blameless when You judge. Behold we were brought forth in iniquity and in sin our mother conceived us, and behold You desire truth in the inward parts, in the hidden parts You will make us to know wisdom. Purge us with hyssop, we shall be clean, wash us and we shall be whiter than snow. Make us to know Your joy and gladness that the bones that You have broken may rejoice and hide Your face from our sins, and blot out our iniquities. Create in us a clean heart O'God and renew a steadfast spirit within us and do not cast us away from Your Presence. Please do not take Your Holy Spirit from us but restore to us the joy of Your salvation and uphold us by Your generous Spirit that we would be able to teach transgressors Your ways and sinners can be converted to You. Deliver us from any blood guiltiness, God of our salvation, and our tongue shall sing aloud of Your Righteousness. Lord open our lips and our mouths shall show forth Your praise. For God does not desire sacrifice or else we would give it, God doesn't delight in burnt offerings. The acceptable sacrifices of God are a humble spirit, a broken and contrite heart. These God will not despise. Do good in Your good pleasure to Zion. Build thou the walls of Jerusalem, then Lord, You will be pleased with the sacrifices of righteousness. I (we) humble myself (ourselves) in complete repentance before You. I/we ask you to forgive me (or us) for any unrighteousness, fornication, wickedness, covetousness, maliciousness, envy, murder, deceit, hatred, whisperers, backbiters, despitefulness, pride, boasters, inventors of evil things, disobedient to parents, being without understanding, covenant breaker(s), without natural affection, homosexuality, unmerciful, injustices, whoredoms, bitterness, evil, evil reasoning, murmuring, doing evil, with no covenant, no love and no peace, argumentive and causing strife. Oh Lord, I/We ask You to forgive each of us of our sins, transgressions, iniquities, trespasses, unforgiveness, approving the sins of others, and I/we ask You to cover those sins with the blood of Jesus Christ. Father I/we truly repent for our sins. Heavenly Father, I/we ask You not to turn us over to a reprobate mind. I/we know that those who commit, practice and approve of those sins without repentance are worthy of death according to Romans 1:32. Please forgive us Lord, in Jesus Name we pray, according to Psalms 51 and Romans 1:32, Amen.

Apostolic Prayer

Dear God, Heavenly Father, We thank You for giving us the Key to the House of David, according to Isaiah 22:22. We take authority and we use this key to close off, lock, shut and seal with the Blood of our Lord and Savior Jesus Christ, all doors, portals, entry ways, windows, and openings, that any curse, demonic assignments, satanic activities, or lies of the enemy can come through to us or the people we pray for. Now Heavenly Father we use the Key to the House of David to open all doors, portals, entry ways, and windows of blessings over us, our children, grandchildren, friends, families, prayer partners and everyone else we pray for. We ask you, Heavenly Father, to post angels around the openings of blessings to keep them open so that the blessings of Heaven flow to us unhindered at all times.

Father God, we thank You for Your mercy, goodness and grace. We pray Your Will be done in all things. In Jesus Mighty Name we pray, Amen.

Daily Warfare Prayer (Out Loud)

Heavenly Father, I come to You in the Name of my Lord and Savior, Jesus Christ. I come to You with praise and thanksgiving, in worship, in humbleness and through the Blood of my Lord and Savior, Jesus Christ of Nazareth. Holy Spirit I ask You to quicken me to my Heavenly Father's Voice and reveal to me any un-confessed sins that I may have in my heart at any time. ______, ______, ______. Heavenly Father, I ask You to forgive me, every member of my family, every partner of Christian Word Ministries, every member of their families, from all sins known or unknown, and transgressions, iniquities, trespasses, any grudges or unforgiveness that we have in our hearts at this time, and wash each of us clean with the Precious Blood of Jesus Christ. Lord Jesus, I ask You to destroy any witchcraft prayers, charismatic witchcraft prayers, psychic prayers, side effects, stings, and influences of any witchcraft prayers that have been prayed over us. I ask You to destroy any hexes, vexes, curses, incantations, chains, fetters, snares, or traps and all of their effects, side affects, adverse effects that have been placed on any of us. I ask You to destroy any assignments, plans or works that satan has against us. I ask You to cause Your anointing to break and destroy the yoke of every bondage that is over us. Lord Jesus, I ask You to pull down and destroy all demonic strongholds, vain imaginations, and every high thought that exalts itself against the knowledge of God, and bring every thought captive to the obedience of Christ according to 2nd Corinthians 10:3-6, in each of us. Lord Jesus I (we) ask You to destroy every demonic spell, witchcraft spell, voodoo spell, black magic spell, white magic spell and all their side effects in each of us. Lord Jesus, I ask you to destroy every false prophecy that has ever been prophesied over us. Lord Jesus I ask You to do all these things according to John 14:14 in the Name of the Lord Jesus Christ of Nazareth. Heavenly Father, I ask You to give us and every person that I pray for today; total deliverance, total freedom, total liberty, total salvation, from all sickness, diseases, infirmities, afflictions, infections, viruses, abnormal cells, radical cells, organs, glands, muscles, ligaments, and bones and I ask You this, according to John 16:23. Heavenly Father, I plead the Blood of Jesus Christ over us and everybody I pray for today, our houses, cars, offices, and properties, as our protection and ask You, Heavenly Father, I ask You to fill each of us and everyone I pray for today, with Your Holy Spirit. Heavenly Father, please help us to keep our eyes fixed on our Savior Jesus Christ and to know that through Him we are victorious. Heavenly Father, I ask You to release Your healing virtue into our bodies and to give us divine health. Heavenly Father, I ask You to give us all these things according to John 16:23. Lord Jesus I ask that You touch everyone I have prayed for today and loose and encamp Your warring angels and ministering angels into our presence, the presence of our houses, cars, offices, properties and pets to force out, drive out, clean out, all evil, wicked, demonic, lying and perverse spirits and prevent any demonic curses, false prophecies, demonic assaults, from entering into our presence. I ask You to force them to go wherever You, want to send them Lord. Heavenly Father, I ask You to bless and prosper me, these people I have been praying and interceding for and our families and anybody we have prayed for today. Lord Jesus, I ask You to continue to bless and prosper each and every one of us in You, Your Word and all that You are, according to John 14:14, to God be the Glory. Amen!

Repentance For A Wrong Attitude

Lord Jesus Christ I ask You to forgive me for the sin of grumbling and complaining, for not walking in faith, and living to the destiny that I have. Lord Jesus Christ my whining attitude is a thing of the past, I am going to rejoice in the Lord, I am going to accept the mind of Christ, I am going to talk about good things, glorious things, God's things, I am going to live with joy unspeakable and full of glory and it is going to begin today, in Jesus Name, amen.

Forgiveness of Others Prayer

Heavenly Father, I forgive anyone who has ever wronged me or hurt me or cursed me or lied to me or prayed witchcraft prayers over me and I bless them in the Name of Jesus Christ. Heavenly Father I ask You to forgive me for any unforgiveness, any bitterness, any anger, any strife, any animosity, and any resentment that I have in my heart toward anyone at this time, in Jesus Name I pray. Amen.

Let the Glory of the Lord Arise

Heavenly Father, I (we) ask that You let the Glory of the Lord rise upon each of us, according to Isaiah 60 verse 2. We ask You Lord to arise over each of us and let Your Glory be seen on each of us. Heavenly Father we ask You to cover each of us with Your Glory and Your Presence.

Daily Prayer For A Child

Heavenly Father, I pray that you will forgive me and every member of my family and all of my friends for anything we have done wrong. Lord help me to forgive anyone who may have hurt me and help anyone that I may have hurt or upset to forgive me. Lord, help me to love others and do what you want me to do. Please come into my heart Lord, and wash away my sins. Lord, help my family to be happy and love one another and not be sad or mad at each other. Dear Lord, please take care of my loved ones and protect and love them as they care for me. I thank you for this wonderful day. Please show my family how much You love them and that you will always be there for them. Teach us to always come to you in prayer. Lord, I pray that every member of my family and all of my friends will accept You into their hearts so that they will go to heaven. Lord Jesus, heal the sick so they will live a long, happy and healthy life. Lord, keep every member of my family, principals, teachers, friends, classmates, and pets safe from any harm or evil. Help me Lord to get good grades in school. Lord Jesus, I pray you protect the President, the leaders of our country and state, and their families. Lord, keep our pastors, firemen, policemen, ambulance drivers, emergency workers and all the soldiers, safe as they do their jobs. I pray for the poor and hungry. Send people to help them and give them a place to sleep, and if they are sick please make them well and feel better. Lord I ask you to visit the sick in the hospitals and prisons, please heal them, and tell them about Your Son, Jesus Christ. Lord Jesus, I ask you to bless everyone that I have prayed for today and send Your mighty angels to protect all of us. Please help us to know you better, Lord Jesus, and have more of you Lord, in our hearts. I pray Lord, that you will be with everyone that I have prayed for today so they will be able to know and love You the way I love You. In Jesus Name I pray. Amen

Prayer For Youth and Teenagers to Pray

Heavenly Father, I know Lord Jesus that You are My Lord and my King, and You intercede for me. You are a loving and forgiving God and I ask You Lord to forgive me for all my sins and any un-forgiveness that I may have in my heart. I ask You Lord to forgive me for not always making You a priority in my life. I know You are strong and I need Your help right now. I am being tempted to do things that are not good for me. Give me strength to say no to these pressures. Help me to find good and Godly things to keep me busy in place of the things that my friends want me to do. You are my strength, Lord. I know, Lord, that You understand all the temptations that face teenagers today and what it will take to keep me from being lured in the wrong direction. So, Lord, I trust in You to know my heart and keep me from these worldly traps. Help me Lord to receive fully, with understanding, Your Word in James 1:3-4, so that when my faith is tested, my endurance has a chance to grow. I know that You will guide me along the right pathway for my life and that You will advise me and watch over me. I know Lord that You are my counselor and that I should always depend on You. I am in need of Your guidance. I don't know what to do (Psalm 32:8). Help me to do what You want done in all situations that I, as a teenager must face. Please Lord, put godly people in my path to show me the steps I need to take. I know Lord that there are friends who destroy each other, but a real friend sticks closer than a brother (Proverbs 18:24). I ask You, Lord to help me find the kind of Christian friends that will be closer than a brother. Help me Lord to be the kind of friend to others that I would want for myself. Open my eyes to see the good qualities in people around me. There are so many questions that I need to ask and I am tom between finding the truth, and having a good time and keeping my friends. I want to do the right thing instead of wearing a mask and being a phony just to be popular. Heavenly Father, I ask for You to show me Your Face when I feel like giving up. Remind me of Your unconditional love when I seem to have no hope in me. I know Lord that You will continue the battle for me when

I can't. I want to learn to cling to You when I am going in the wrong direction. Help me to keep my thoughts on You when I become weak. Help me to continue to praise You during these low times. I thank You, Heavenly Father, for reaching down into my world and drawing me close to You. Thank You for allowing me to soak up Your strength during moments like these. I thank you Lord for never giving up on me, even when I've given up on myself. Make me into the worthwhile person you destined me to be. Teach me to know Your Will for my life and to be obedient to You. Do not let anything Lord interfere with Your destiny for my life. I know You have a great plan for me help me to find it. I praise You Lord for the comfort that You bring by just listening to me. In Jesus Name I pray. Amen.

Curses

The Word of God says that a curse without a cause can not settle on a righteous person. Sin opens the door (primarily disobedience) for a curse to settle on a person. Generational curses are curses in which a parent or ancestral parent that we are in direct lineage of, has sinned and opened a door for it to be passed on from one generation to the next. Usually there is some type of display or manifestation in the natural realm, indicating what the curse is, through a person's behavior. No matter how pronounced the manifestation is, it needs to be dealt with through repentance. A curse without a cause cannot settle on a righteous person or a person free of sin. Curses are clearly spoken of in the Bible and just because the Word tells us Jesus became a curse on a tree for us does not mean we can't still get a curse actively working in our lives. We either get curses through our sin or when we get into sin, a curse spoken of by others gets attached to us after we sin, actively affecting us. We need to repent immediately! These things really do affect our thoughts and the thought processes of our mind more than we tend to realize! With generational curses, we also repent for our own sins and also the sins of our ancestors. No matter the sin, and no matter the type of curse, we need to ask the Lord to take it and break it from us. Then we are appropriating and applying what Jesus did for us by going to the cross and becoming a curse for us.

Prayer Breaking Curses

Heavenly Father I come to You now in the Name of my Lord and Savior Jesus Christ. Holy Spirit I ask You to quicken me and lead me in prayer. Lord Jesus, I believe that on the cross You took upon Yourself every curse that could and would ever come against me. Lord Jesus, I ask You to destroy every curse that is on me at this time, on my children, my grandchildren, ______, ______, and ______ at this time, including those whose names are ______, ______ and ______, according to Thy Will. Lord Jesus, I (we) ask You to break and destroy any curses, ungodly soul ties, unholy alliances or any unrighteous agreements that I (we) have entered into. Destroy any side effects, effects, residual effects, influences or stings of any curses that have been put on me (us), placed on me (us), declared over me (us), decreed over me (us), anyone that I (we) have prayed for today, including our children, our grandchildren, our marriages, our homes, our cars, our trucks, our offices, our properties, our buildings, our businesses, our ministries, and our finances. I (we) ask You to do this in the Name of Jesus Christ of Nazareth according to John 14:14. I (we) ask You to destroy any witchcraft prayers, charismatic witchcraft prayers, psychic prayers, ungodly soulish prayers, side effects, effects, residual effects, influences, or stings of any witchcraft prayers or charismatic witchcraft prayers or psychic prayers, ungodly soulish prayers about me (us), over, or about anyone that I (we) have prayed for today, including our children, our grandchildren, our marriages, our homes, our cars, our trucks, our offices, our properties, our buildings, our businesses, our ministries, our finances, our pets . . . . I (we) ask You to destroy them now in the Name of Jesus Christ of Nazareth according to John 14:14. I (we) ask You to destroy any false prophecies that have been prophesied over me (us), or about me (us), or anyone that I (we) have prayed for today, including our children, our grandchildren, our marriages, our homes, our cars, our trucks, our offices, our properties, our buildings, our businesses, our ministries, our finances . . . . I (we) ask You to destroy them now in the Name of Jesus Christ of Nazareth according to John 14:14. Lord Jesus, I (we) ask You to destroy any hexes, vexes, witchcraft spells, voodoo spells, satanic spells, incantations, chains, fetters, snares, traps, effects, side effects, or residual effects, darts, arrows, stings, claws, spears, darkness, evil imprints, false memories, wrong mind sets, trauma, shock, any unrighteous instruments of the enemy that have attempted to penetrate me (us), any lies of the enemy, false memories, evil imprints, impressions, wrong thoughts and mind sets, that have been spoken into me (us), over me (us), anyone that I (we) have prayed for today, including our children, our grandchildren, our marriages, our homes, our cars, our trucks, our offices, our properties, our buildings, our businesses, our ministries, our finances . . . . I (we) ask You to destroy them now in the Name of Jesus Christ of Nazareth according to John 14:14. Lord Jesus, I ask You to destroy any words, declarations, decrees, effects, side effects, stings and influences that have been spoken into me (us) or over me (us), or into anyone or over anyone that I (we) have prayed for today by ourselves or others that do not conform to Your will or Your destiny for our lives or the way You want us to believe and think and do. I apply the Blood of Jesus Christ of Nazareth, His Blood Covenant, Psalms 91, and Your healing virtue over me (us), into me (us), my spirit, mind, will, desires, emotions, ego, imaginations, anyone I (we) prayed for today.

In the Name of the Lord Jesus Christ of Nazareth, I (we) ask You Lord Jesus to destroy any assignments or plans that satan or our spiritual enemies or physical enemies have against me (us), anyone that I (we) have prayed for today, against our children, our grandchildren, our marriages, our homes, our cars, our trucks, our offices, our properties, our finances, our buildings, our businesses, our ministries . . . etc. I (we) ask You to destroy them now in the Name of Jesus Christ of Nazareth according to John 14:14. To God be the Glory. Amen!

In the Name of the Lord Jesus Christ of Nazareth, I (we) ask You Lord Jesus to pull down and cast aside every demonic stronghold that is in my (our) mind(s) or that are in the minds of anyone that I (we) have prayed for today. I (we) ask You to pull down every vain imagination in me (us) and in everyone that I (we) pray for today and cast them aside in the Name of the Lord Christ Jesus. Lord Jesus, I (we) ask You to pull down every high thought in me (us) and in everyone that I (we) have prayed for today; that exalts itself against the knowledge of God and cast them aside in the Name of the Lord Jesus Christ of Nazareth and to bring every thought captive in each of us to the obedience of Christ Jesus according to 2 Corinthians 10:3-6. Lord Christ Jesus, I (we) ask You to pull down, cast aside and destroy any demonic strongholds that are over or in me (us), or over or in anyone that I (we) have prayed for today; over our homes, cars, trucks, offices, property, buildings, businesses, ministries, marriages, finances. I (we) ask You to destroy them now according to John 14:14 in the Name of the Lord Jesus Christ of Nazareth. To God be the Glory. Amen! In the Name of my Lord and Savior Jesus Christ, I command my mind, desires, will, emotions, ego, imaginations, and thoughts, to come now to the obedience of Christ in me. Lord Jesus I ask You to destroy and remove all vain imaginations, demonic strongholds, and any deception that is in my thoughts and mind, and cast them aside in the Name of Jesus Christ. I ask You to wash my (our) mind(s) clean with the Precious Blood of Jesus Christ of Nazareth and enable me (us) to stay in Your Presence all day long, according to John 14:14, to God be the glory! Amen. Lord Jesus, Your Word says that Your anointing destroys all yokes of bondage (Isaiah 10:27) so I (we) ask You now to cause Your anointing to break and destroy any yokes of bondages along with all of their works, roots, fruits, tentacles and links that are in my (our) life (lives), the lives of anyone that I (we) have prayed for today according to John 14:14, in the Name of the Lord Jesus Christ, to God be the Glory. Amen!

Blessing Prayer

Heavenly Father, I (we) come to You now in the Name of my (our) Lord and Savior Christ Jesus. Heavenly Father, I (we) ask

You to give me (us) divine healing now in every area of my (our) life, spirit, mind, will, emotions and physical being in accordance with Your Divine Plan and Order for my (our) life. I (we) receive Your Divine Healing, Wholeness and Newness of life(s), in the Name of Jesus Christ. Lord, I (we) ask You to expand in me (us) Your territories. Lord I (we) ask for and receive beauty for ashes, the oil of joy for mourning, the garment of praise for the spirit of heaviness: for I (we) are trees of righteousness, the planting of the Lord, that You may be glorified, in Jesus' Name. Thy will be done on earth as it is in Heaven, Father, I (we) pray with thanksgiving in Jesus' Name. Amen! Heavenly Father, I ask you to give me (us) and every person I (we) prayed for today according to John 16:23, the manifestation of every miracle and every healing You have given to me (us) and the manifestation of divine healing and divine health in my (each of our) body (ies). Amen!

Blessings: Heavenly Father, I (we) come to You now in the Name of my (our) Lord and Savior Christ Jesus.

Lord Jesus Christ, I (we) ask You, according to John 14:13—14, to cover me (us) with Your anointing, glory, and tangible Presence, give me (us) a fresh new release and flow in my (our) inner man with rivers of living waters springing up forth abundantly with Life abundant, fill me (us) to over-flowing with Your favor, compassion and love, Your wisdom and understanding. Anoint me (us) to hear Your Voice not that of a stranger, cause me (us) to clearly discern Your Voice over that of a strange voice. Give me (us) Your eyes to see spiritually, and a heart to understand and be led by Your Holy Spirit, clearly, help me to be bold, confident and be obedient, to do Your will. Fill me (us) with Your gifts, anointings, and blessings and all else You have for me (us). Lord Jesus Christ I (we) ask You according to John 14:13—14 to anoint me (us). Pour out Your Anointing on me (us). (Apply the anointing oil to the forehead now.) I (we) receive Your Anointing in the Name of the Father, the Son, and the Holy Spirit. Lord Jesus Christ, I (we) ask You, according to John 14:13—14, to do all these things and let Your love so brightly shine through me (us) into others and as an act of worship to You, in Jesus' Name, to God be the Glory. Amen!

Prayer Binding and Loosing Demonic Spirits

Heavenly Father, according to Matthew 16 and 18, I thank you that whatsoever I shall bind on earth shall be bound in Heaven and whatsoever I loose on earth shall be loosed in Heaven.

In the Name of the Lord Jesus Christ of Nazareth, I (we) bind all of satan's evil, wicked, demon, lying and tormenting spirits and strongmen along with all evil principalities, powers and rulers of wickedness in high places; including all their works, roots, fruits, tentacles and links including any spirits and strongmen of doubt, unbelief, leviathan, pride, anger, rage, strife, deception, self-deception, confusion, self-confusion, divination, Jezebel, Python, accusation, familiar spirits, delusion, self-delusion, unforgiveness, witchcraft, and willful sins: ______, ______, and ______. (Please look at the demon list on page 37; and loose any foul spirits that you feel may apply to you.) I (we) bind and loose all these demonic spirits and strongmen from me (us), from everyone that I (we) have prayed for today, from every organ in our bodies, from every cell in our bodies, from every gland, muscle, ligament and bone in our bodies, from our homes, properties, marriages, cars, trucks, businesses, ministries, objects, work places, finances, pets . . . and I (we) loose them to go where Jesus sends them and I (we) bind them and command them to stay there; in the Name of Jesus Christ of Nazareth. I (we) place the Blood of the Lord Christ Jesus between us.

Heavenly Father, it is written in Psalms 91, and Matthew 6, and many other places of Your Word that You are my (our) Deliverer and I (we) ask that You give me (us), and everyone that I (we) prayed for today: total deliverance, total freedom, total liberty, and total salvation from all evil, wicked, demon, lying, perverse, unclean, foul, demonic spirits, strongmen, and their messengers, and from all sicknesses, diseases, infirmities, afflictions, infections, viruses, inflammations, disorders of any kind in every cell in our bodies, in every gland in our bodies, in every organ in our bodies, abnormal cells, radical cells, abnormal growths, radical growths, cancers, tumors, spasms, lesions, or cysts in any parts of our bodies. Heavenly Father, I (we) ask You to give our homes, cars, trucks, offices, businesses, finances, ministries, properties and pets: total deliverance and liberty and freedom from all evil, wicked, lying, perverse and unclean spirits in the Name of Jesus Christ. I (we) thank You for giving me (us) this deliverance, freedom, liberty and salvation from all these things in the Name of the Lord Jesus Christ of Nazareth. Heavenly Father, I ask You to give me (us) and each person I (we) pray for today divine healing, divine health, and the manifestation of every miracle and every healing that you have ever given me (us) according to John 16:23. May these deliverances be used to glorify You, Heavenly Father. In the Name of the Lord Jesus Christ of Nazareth, I (we) command our minds, wills, and emotions to submit to the obedience of Christ in me (us). To God be the Glory. Amen!

Applying the Blood of Jesus Prayer

Heavenly Father, I (we) bow and worship and praise before You and I (we) apply the Blood of Jesus Christ over myself (ourselves), each person that I (we) have prayed for today; from the tops of our heads to the soles of our feet. I (we) apply the Blood of Jesus over each of us, over the airways that surround us, over us and under us, over telephone lines, over our homes, properties, offices, cars, trucks, businesses, finances, marriages, ministries, cell phone frequencies, and I (we) ask You to render powerless and harmless and nullify the power, destroy the power, cancel the power of any evil spirit, demonic spirit, demonic strongman, messenger of Satan and witchcraft prayer that tries to come into our presence, our homes, everything in our homes, our pets, our properties, our cars, our trucks, everything in our cars and trucks, our marriages, our finances, our ministries, our telephone lines, our telephone frequencies . . . in the Name of Jesus Christ of Nazareth.

Lord Jesus Christ, I (we) ask You to wash and cleanse my (our) mind(s) with Your Precious Blood. Give each of us clarity of thought; give each of us a sound and sober mind, in Jesus Christ Holy Name; according to John 14:14. To God be the Glory. Amen!

Filled with the Holy Spirit Prayer

Heavenly Father, I (we) ask You to fill each of us with Your precious Holy Spirit. I (we) ask You to fill each of us with all of the fruits of Your Holy Spirit including Your love, Your joy, Your peace, Your gentleness, Your goodness, Your meekness, Your faithfulness and Your self-control. Heavenly Father, in Christ Jesus' Holy Name I (we) ask You to fill me (us), everyone I (we) prayed for today with Your Holy Ghost anointing and power, cover us with Your presence, Your anointing, Your power; in the Name of Jesus Christ of Nazareth and I (we) ask You Lord Jesus to heal me (us) and fill me (us) with Your Holy Spirit and power, cover us with Your anointing and presence, and to fill me (us) and seal me (us) with Your peace, character, and nature. I (we) ask You to do all these things in the Name of the Lord Jesus Christ of Nazareth according to John 14:14. To God be the Glory. Amen!

Binding the Enemies Eyes and Ears Prayer

In the Name of the Lord Jesus Christ of Nazareth, I (we) bind all of satan's evil, wicked, demon, lying, unclean, perverse tormenting spirits and strongmen and messengers, their eyes blind, their ears deaf to our prayers, conversations and actions in the Name of the Lord Christ Jesus unless we speak directly to them. I (we) bind them and command them not to manifest in my (our) presence, the presence of anyone that I am (we are) around today, the presence of anyone that I (we) have prayed for today; or in the presence of our homes, cars, trucks, offices, properties, buildings, businesses, ministries, marriages, finances. Heavenly Father, I (we) ask that You shut any doors that need to be shut and open any doors that need to be opened in the spiritual and natural realms of our lives in Jesus' Holy Name. Heavenly Father, I apply the Blood of Jesus over those doorways and ask that the enemy be rendered powerless and harmless so they cannot come back through those doorways ever again to our homes, properties, cars, trucks, work places, businesses, finances, minds, ministries, our spouses, spouse's work places, our children, their schools, their work places, our friends and loved ones in Jesus Christ's Holy Name. To God be the Glory. Amen!

Armor of God Prayer

Heavenly Father, I am (we are) thankful for Your mighty armor You have provided for us. I (we) put on us the full armor of God: the Helmet of Salvation; the Breastplate of Righteousness; the Girdle of Truth; Sandals of Peace; the Shield of Faith which protects (guards) us from all fiery darts of the enemy; and I (we) pick up the Sword of the Spirit, the Word of God that I (we) choose to use against all the forces of evil in our lives. I (we) place on our feet the Sandals of Peace of the Lord Jesus Christ of the Kingdom of God. I (we) ask You Lord according to John 14:13-14, to be our Guard and a Shield about us. Take us into the cleft of the Rock and underneath Your Mighty Wings according to Psalms 91. I (we) put Your Armor on us and live and pray in complete dependence upon You, and pray in the Spirit at all times and on all occasions. (Ephesians 6:10-18) Blessed Heavenly Father. To God be the Glory. Amen!

Angels For Protection Prayer

According to John 14:14 I (we) ask You Lord Jesus to loose Your angels in great abundance in my (our) presence, the presence of everyone I (we) have prayed for today and into our homes, cars, trucks, lands, properties, buildings, and work places to protect us, guard us, and to force out, drive out and to cleanse out all evil, wicked, demon and tormenting spirits from our presence, and our homes, cars, trucks, lands, properties, animals, and work places and force them into the Abyss and any replacement thereof, and they cannot return to us. Lord Jesus I (we) ask You to create a hedge of protection of angels around each of our minds and loose Your Mighty and Warring angels around each of us, our homes, cars, trucks, lands, properties, animals, and work places to protect us from the enemy, I ask You to do this according to John 14:14, in Christ Jesus' Holy Name, to God be the Glory, amen!

Thank You For Your Promise

Father, I come to You in the Name of Jesus, my Lord, my Savior. I come to You with a heart of thanksgiving. I thank you for all the good things in my life, for You are the Creator of all things good. Father, I thank You for Your Presence. For in Your Presence is the fullness of my joy and in Your Presence I am complete and whole. In Your Presence I have purpose. Because of Your Presence, I am glad to be here. Father, I thank You for Your plan, that I might have a full life and enjoy it and have it in abundance to overflowing. Father, I thank You for Your provision, that all my needs are met according to Your riches in glory and that I may prosper in all areas of my life as my soul prospers. Father, I thank You for Your protection, that Your perfect love casteth out all fear and that no weapon formed against me shall prosper. Father, I thank You for Your peace. The peace that passes all understanding. The peace that keeps me calm and secure through adversity. The peace that leads me through all the storms that come into my life. Father, thank You for my life and Your Presence in it. In Jesus Name. Amen.

Psalms 91 Protection Prayer

Heavenly Father, I (we) come to You now in the Name of my (our) Lord and Savior Christ Jesus, I (we) make a joyful shout to You, we come before Your Presence with singing, and we enter into Your gates with thanksgiving, and into Your courts with praise, and You are good from everlasting to everlasting. Lord throughout this prayer and throughout this day I pray for myself (ourselves) and the following people, ______, ______, ______, and ______. I (we) pray for myself (ourselves), everyone that I (we) prayed for today. I (we) pray for all members of congress and of the armed forces of our nation, all of our intercessors, teachers, pastors, friends, enemies, neighbors, doctors, dentists, all people of Israel, everyone we go to church with, and all of Your workers. Heavenly Father, I (we) ask You to let us dwell in the secret place of the most High and abide under the shadow of the Almighty. I (we) ask You to let us say that You are our Lord, our refuge, our fortress and our God in whom we can trust. I (we) ask You to deliver us from the snare of the fowler, and from the deadly pestilence. I (we) ask You to cover each of us with Your feathers and let us walk under Your wings to take refuge. I (we) ask You to let Your faithfulness and truth be our shield and armor. I (we) ask You to let us not be afraid of the terror by night; nor for the arrow that flieth by day; nor for the deadly pestilence that walketh in darkness nor for the destruction that wasteth at noonday. I (we) ask You to cause a thousand to fall at our side, and ten thousand at our right hand and not to let any come near us. I (we) ask You to give Your angels charge over us to keep us in all Your ways and let Your angel's hands lift us up, so we do not even dash our foot against a stone or be hurt in any way. I (we) ask You to let us tread upon the lion and serpent and to let us trample the young lion and the serpent under our feet. I (we) ask You Heavenly Father, to answer us when we call upon You, be with us in trouble, deliver us, honor us and satisfy us with a long life and show us Your salvation. Heavenly Father, I (we) thank You that these things are written in Psalms 91, that we can dwell in the secret place of the most High, and I (we) thank You that we can abide under the shadow of our Almighty God. I (we) thank You that we can say You are our Lord, our refuge, our fortress and our God, whom we can trust. I (we) thank You for delivering us from the snare of the fowler, and from the deadly pestilence. I (we) thank You for covering each of us with Your feathers. I (we) thank You that we can walk under Your wings and take refuge. I (we) thank You that Your faithfulness and truth is our shield and armor, I (we) thank You that we are not afraid for the terror by night nor for the arrow that flieth by day; nor for the pestilence that walketh in darkness; nor for the destruction that wasteth at noonday. I (we) thank You that a thousand shall fall at our side, and ten thousand at our right hand and none will come near us. I (we) thank You for giving Your angels charge over us to keep us in all ways and that Your angel's hands will lift us up so we do not dash our foot against a stone. I (we) thank You that we can tread upon the lion and serpent and trample the young lion and the dragon under our feet. I (we) thank You that when we call upon You, You will answer us, and be with us in trouble. Deliver us, honor us, satisfy us with a long life and show us Your salvation. Heavenly Father, I am (we are) thankful that our Lord Christ Jesus spoiled all principalities and powers and made a show of them openly and triumphed over them in Himself. I (we) claim all that victory for our lives. I (we) reject all the insinuations, accusations, and temptations of satan. I (we) affirm that the Word of God is true and we choose to live in obedience to You Lord Jesus and in fellowship with You. Open our eyes and show us the areas of our lives that do not please You. Work in us to cleanse us from all ground that would give satan a foothold against us. We do in every way stand in all that it means to be your adopted child and we welcome all the ministry of Your Holy Spirit. Heavenly Father, I (we) pray that now and through our lives, You would strengthen and enlighten us, show us the way satan and his demonic spirits are trying to hinder, tempt, lie, and distort the truth in our lives. Enable us to be the kind of person that will please you. Enable us to be aggressive in prayer and faith. Enable us to be aggressive mentally, to think about and practice Your word, and to give You, Your rightful place in our lives. Heavenly Father, I (we) place all of my (our) cares, all of my (our) anxieties, all of my (our) worries and all of my (our) concerns once and for all on You, because I (we) know that You love me (us) and watch over me (us) according to 1 Peter 5:7. Heavenly Father, I (we) pray for the peace of Jerusalem and may all those prosper who love You. Psalms 122:6. Heavenly Father, I (we) pray that You will establish Jerusalem and make her a praise in the earth. Isaiah 62:7. To God be the Glory. Amen!

Prayer Against Demons that Follow

Heavenly Father, I come to You in Jesus Christ's Holy Name. I ask You Lord Jesus Christ according to John 14:13 & 14, that any evil spirits that are following me and/or ______, ______, and ______ that You would force and drive those evil spirits into the Abyss and any replacements of evil spirits, destroy their assignments and attacks against me, and ______, ______, and ______. Lord Jesus, force and drive those evil spirits far from our houses, cars, lands, properties, vehicles, animals, and work places, and do not let them return anywhere near us the rest of this day and into tomorrow, in Jesus Name we pray. Amen.

Prayer to destroy Unrighteous Agreements

Heavenly Father, I come to You in Jesus Christ's Holy Name. I ask You Lord Jesus Christ according to John 14:13 & 14, that You destroy the unrighteous agreements that are coming against me that have been prayed, are being prayed, or will be prayed, any replacements thereof, throughout the rest of this day, through the night watches, and into tomorrow afternoon, along with their effects, side effects, and stings. I ask You Lord to destroy all demonic spirits that have been sent forth from those words and/or prayers and cast them into the Abyss, along with those words, the power of those words and/or prayers, any pain, darkness, darts, arrows, stings, claws, spears, lies, evil imprints, impressions, false memories, wrong mindsets, throughout the rest of this day, the night watches, and into tomorrow afternoon, Amen.

Declaration For the Coming Storm (Pastor John Kilpatrick)

Brother (Sister), let not your hearts be troubled. Be it known this day that the Hand of the Lord rests upon you and your seed. I declare that you are the blessed of the Lord and that the blessing of the Lord shall search you out and find you to bestow upon you God's bounty I proclaim that you will see with your eyes the reward of the wicked. But because you have made the Lord your refuge, even the Most High your habitation, there shall no evil befall you; neither shall any plague come nigh your dwelling. God has given His angels charge over you to keep you in all your ways. God declares that He will deliver you and set you on high. You will call, and He will answer. He will be with you in trouble and will honor you. You shall have long life, and you shall see the salvation of the Lord. I declare, proclaim, and decree that this house shall be a "Goshen": a place of safety, a place of security, a harbor of peace of rare abundance, and a house of more than enough. Your alms shall be remembered as a memorial before the Lord. Your love for Israel (both the land and God's people, the Jews) will not go unrewarded. The heavens are open over this place and this people. Let not your hearts fear or tremble. God is not a man that He should lie, but His Word is sure, and it will surely come to pass with every benefit and blessing He promised. Now the Lord Bless you in Jesus Name! Go in peace.

Blessing to Pray Over Others (Pastor John Kilpatrick)

"God's" blessings rest upon You this day. You are pleasing to the Lord and He enjoys your fellowship. You are well-favored and more than able to receive His abundant provision. God's angels accompany you on your right hand and on your left. They shall guide you! God's goodness and mercy shall follow close behind you and be the guardians between you and your past. God has determined that you shall have good success because you move in faith and in strong courage. Your eyes shall see the salvation of the Lord. He shall keep you safely under His wings and pinions. I declare this day that you are protected and delivered from the evil of the day. You shall not stumble or fall for the Holy Spirit has anointed your eyes with eye salve to see clearly and has given you ears of the spirit to hear precisely. You will be wise in your generation. Your soul will rest in God's shalom. He has declared you to be strong and pleasing! in His sight. You will eat the fruit of his promises in the land of the living and will enjoy long life and length of days because you have wholly trusted in the Lord your God. Your habitation shall be a place where you will rest in His love, find hope for tomorrow, and joy shall strengthen you as you rest upon your bed. He shall restore your soul and give you rest in the stillness and quietness of your home. In your prayer chamber the Holy Spirit shall birth a creative and powerful mind and give you sound ideas that will bring you promotion and great favor. He shall give you fresh anointings and bless your ministry with good results. The Lord is pleased with you and has placed His name upon your forehead. Call upon Him and He will show you great and mighty things you know not of. I bless you in Jesus' Name!"

Deuteronomy 28 Blessing Prayer

Heavenly Father, I (we) ask You to bless us when we come in. I (we) ask You to bless us when we go out. I (we) ask You to bless us in the city. I (we) ask You to bless us in the country. I (we) ask You to bless our fruits. I (we) ask You to bless our seed. I (we) ask You to bless our land. I (we) ask You to bless our store house. I ask You to bless and prosper everything we touch. I (we) ask You to cause our enemies to come at us in one direction but to flee from us in seven directions because greater are You who is in us than he that is in the world. To God be the Glory, according to Your Will, amen!

Numbers 6:23-26 Blessing Prayer

Heavenly Father, in Christ Jesus' Holy Name; I (we) thank You for Your Word in Numbers 6:23-26. Heavenly Father, I (we) pray that You will bless us and that You will keep us. I pray that You will make Your Face shine upon us and be gracious to us. I pray that You will lift up Your countenance upon us and fill us with Your Peace. Lord Jesus, I (we) thank You for blessing us. Lord Jesus, I (we) ask You destroy false memories, lies of the enemy, unrighteous agreements, bad attitudes, bad thoughts, ungodly negative impressions, and imprints according to John 14:14. Heavenly Father, I (we) ask You to cleanse our minds with the Blood of the Lord Christ Jesus of all thoughts and preconceived ideas that do not conform to Your will and destiny for our lives and the way You want us to believe and think. Lord Jesus, I (we) ask You to prevent our minds from deceiving us in any way. Lord Jesus, I (we) ask you to do all of these things according to John 14:14; and Heavenly Father I (we) ask You to give us these things according to John 16:23. In the Name of the Lord Jesus Christ of Nazareth, I (we) pray with thanksgiving. To God be the Glory. Amen!

Daily Commitment of Your Will in Life to the Lord

Heavenly Father I come to You in Jesus Christ's Holy Name, I renew and give my total allegiance to You, Lord Jesus Christ, Father God and Holy Spirit, fresh and a new, today and for the rest of my life, to do Your work, to do Your will and obey You at all times. I give my life, and all that is in it, as a living sacrifice, unto You which is my reasonable service, that first and foremost, all that I am would be a glory, honor, and praise unto You, Heavenly Father, Son, and Holy Spirit, in Jesus Christ's Holy Name. I commit my life and all that is in it, to You, to do Your Good Works, and to have and be in Your Total Desire, Will, and Presence, that I will, I am, and I will be, transformed into Your total likeness in Jesus Christ's Holy Name. Come Lord Jesus Christ take Your rightful place in, through, and about my life. I give my life to You Lord, for eternity and I ask You Lord, to bind all that I am to all that You are, in Jesus Christ's Holy Name. Amen.

Whose Waters Faileth Not And Your Presence With Me

Heavenly Father, I (we) come to You now in the Name of my (our) Lord and Savior Christ Jesus. Holy Spirit I (we) pray that You will quicken me (us) to hear my (our) Heavenly Father's

Voice and lead me (us) in prayer. Heavenly Father, I (we) bow and worship before You. I (we) come to You with praise and with thanksgiving. I (we) come to You in humility, in fear, in trembling and seeking the truth. I (we) come to You in gratitude, in love, and through the precious Blood of Your Son Jesus Christ of Nazareth. Heavenly Father God, I (we) thank You that Your Word says that when I (we) pray to You that You will hear me (us) according to Job 22:27-28. Heavenly Father, Your word says that in every place I (we) go where Your Name is remembered, You will come to me (us) and bless me (us) according to Your word in Exodus 20:24, and Your presence will go with me (us) wherever I (we) go and You will give me (us) rest according to Exodus 33:14. Heavenly Father, I (we) pray that You will continually guide me (us) and satisfy my (our) desires in scorched places, give strength to my (our) bones and I will be like a watered garden and like a spring of water, whose waters do not fail, according to your Word. Isaiah 58:11. Heavenly Father, I (we) pray in the Name of my (our) Lord and Savior Jesus Christ of Nazareth that You would destroy the power of all demonic spirits that are coming against me, ______ and ______, our homes, properties, automobiles, business, finances, ministries. That You would encamp Your angels and chariots of fire all around me (us), according to 2 Kings 6:17-18. Heavenly Father, I (we) declare these things in the Name of the Lord Jesus Christ of Nazareth and I (we) thank You that they will be established for us, according to Job 22:27-28. Amen!

Prayer for Mind Cleansing & Clarity

Heavenly Father, I (we) come to You now in the Name of my (our) Lord and Savior Christ Jesus. Lord Jesus Christ we ask You according to John 14: 13—14, to wash over our minds with the Blood of Jesus and cleanse out all darkness and all thoughts that are contrary to Your will and destiny for our lives. I (we) ask You Lord Jesus to shut any doors that need to be shut whether spiritual or natural, and to open any doors that need to be opened whether spiritual or natural in my (our) life (lives). Heavenly Father, I (we) ask you to give me (us) and each person I (we) have prayed for today clarity of vision, clarity of sight, clarity of thought, clarity of mind, clarity of knowing, and hearing Your Voice according to John 16:23. Amen!

Spiritual Doors Prayer

Heavenly Father, I (we) come to You now in the Name of my (our) Lord and Savior Christ Jesus. Heavenly Father, I (we) ask that You shut any doors that need to be shut in my (our) life (ves) and open any doors that need to be opened, in the spiritual and natural realms of my (our lives) life in Jesus' Holy Name. Heavenly Father, I (we) plead the Blood of Jesus over those doorways and ask that the enemy be rendered powerless and harmless so they can not come back through those doorways ever again to my (our) home, property, automobile, work place, business, finances, ministry, my spouse, spouse's work place, our children, their schools, their work places, our friends and loved ones in Jesus Christ's Holy Name, I (we) pray with thanksgiving, amen.

Resentment and Bitterness Prayer

Heavenly Father, I (we) come to You now in the Name of my (our) Lord and Savior Christ Jesus. Father, help me (us) to let go of all bitterness and resentment. You are the One Who binds up and heals the brokenhearted. I (we) receive Your anointing that breaks and destroys every yoke of bondage. I (we) receive healing by faith according to Your Word, Isaiah 53:5, "and with His stripes we are healed". Thank You for sending me (us) Your Holy Spirit, I (we) acknowledge the Holy Spirit as my (our) wonderful Counselor! Thank You for helping me (us) work out my (our) salvation with fear and trembling, for it is You, Father, Who works in me (us) to will and to act according to Your good purpose.

In the Name of Jesus, I (we) choose to forgive those who have wronged me (us). I (we) choose to live a life of forgiveness because You have forgiven me (us). I (we) repent of all resentments, bitterness, rage, anger, brawling, and slander, along with every form of malice. I (we) desire to be kind and compassionate to others, forgiving them, just as in Christ You forgave me (us). With the help of the Holy Spirit, I (we) make every effort to live in peace with all men and to be holy, for I (we) know that without holiness no one will see You. I (we) will watch and pray that I (we) will not enter into temptation or cause others to stumble. Thank You, Heavenly Father, that You watch over Your Word to perform it and that whom the Son has set free is free indeed. I (we) declare that I (we) have overcome resentment and bitterness by the Blood of the Lord Jesus Christ and by the Word of my (our) testimony. Amen!

Lord Help Me Prayer

We are not moved by what we see, hear, smell, touch or taste. We are not moved by reason. We are only moved by Your Spirit and Your Word and we know Your Voice, and we hear Your Voice and we refuse to follow strangers according to John 10:27. Our seed is mighty upon the earth according to Psalms 112:2. Lord Jesus, I ask you to expand my territories; to fill me and increase me in the Holy Spirit and anointing with power.

I ask You to lead me in paths of righteousness for Your Name's Sake. I Bless You, Praise You, Worship You, and commit all that I am to You, that Your perfect will be done through me.

I ask that You help me to cease from my own labors. I do so by faith.

I ask that You cause me to enter Your Rest now, in Jesus' Name and I receive that.

I ask You to release my warring and ministering angels to minister and war on my behalf.

I ask you to fill this, Your temple; with as much Shikinah Glory as possible.

Help me to bear the cross You have prepared for me and help those in my family.

I ask that the Holy Spirit speak to my heart through Your Word.

I ask that You prepare me with reverence and worship, and with humility through Your Holy Spirit.

I ask that You take out of me, add to me or do to me; anything You want.

I ask that the Word I read would be engrafted into me and become part of me; spirit, mind, will and emotions.

I declare by Your power; You are helping and causing me to be bold, dauntless, fearless, confident, intrepid, valiant, steadfast, faithful, true and loyal for Your Name's Sake.

I ask You to deliver me where I am blind, wretched, naked, and poor. I ask for your help.

I ask You to help me not be the accuser of the brethren but to teach others in gentleness, to be a help in season, to edify, to exhort and comfort others.

I ask for Love and Grace for others and Grace from You Lord. I ask for help that Your Love and Grace in me; flow and be administered to others by Your Spirit in me, to manifest Your Presence in and through me.

I release all things into Your hands and commit myself unto You, trusting You.

I ask for help, that You give me the Word that You want me to give to others.

Lord forgive me and help me to follow Your direction.

I ask that You would send those that would receive the gift of salvation to me, that I may witness to them. Let them ask and receive, Father!

I ask that You give me a clear mind and thoughts toward You, clear will toward You, and clear of all emotional clutter. (This is all about You. Hearing You is easier than thinking!)

I ask that You cause me to hear You louder and clearer, and rest in You.

I ask You to release Your love, joy, peace, patience, kindness, goodness, faithfulness, gentleness, with long-suffering, and self-control to flow over and in and throughout my life. (I ask You to fashion my heart like Yours, that Your fruit will abound in and through me to others.)

I ask You Father for a clear, sharp, and healthy mind and body in You.

Heavenly Father, I ask for Your perfect Will being worked out through my life and the lives of those that my life touch; as You direct me.

I ask You for eyes to see, ears to hear, and a heart to comprehend and receive what the Holy Spirit has to say.

I ask to speak and to do Your perfect will in this life; for You, for me, and for my family.

I ask You to guard me and my family with many angels and that they manifest as needed.

I ask You to make me alert, awake, sharp and attentive in Your thoughts and ways.

I ask that I may prosper in what I put my hands to do for You. I ask you to renew my youth like the eagles. I ask for a heart like Yours and growth and maturity to walk in it to the fullest with You; in Jesus' Name. Amen!

Holy Spirit have Your way with all of me, in Jesus' Name. Amen!

Heavenly Father, I declare Your faithfulness to the heavens and Your loving kindness and tender mercies anew every morning. Amen!

Heavenly Father, I ask that my mind, will and emotions do not deceive me in hearing Your Voice and be still in Jesus' Name.

Heavenly Father, I ask that You shut any doors that need to be shut and open any doors that need to be opened in the spiritual and natural realms in Jesus' Name. Heavenly Father, I plead the blood of Jesus over those doorways and ask that the enemy be rendered powerless and harmless so they can not come back through those doorways ever again; to me, ______, ______, and ______, our houses, lands, properties, vehicles, work places, schools, and finances in Jesus' Name. Amen!

1 Thessalonians 5:23-24 Prayer

Heavenly Father, I (we) come to You now in the Name of my (our) Lord and Savior Christ Jesus. Heavenly Father, I (we) pray for myself (ourselves) and everyone that I (we) prayed for today and I (we) ask that You, the God of peace Himself will sanctify us completely; and that our whole spirit, soul, and body will be preserved blameless at the coming of our Lord and Savior Jesus Christ. I (we) ask You Heavenly Father Who is called Faithful to do it. Amen.

Isaiah 40:31 Prayer

Heavenly Father, I (we) come to You now in the Name of my (our) Lord and Savior Christ Jesus. Heavenly Father, I (we) pray for myself (ourselves) and everyone that I (we) prayed for today and I (we) ask that You will renew our strength, the ones that wait upon You: that we shall mount up with wings like eagles, they we will run and not be weary we will walk and not faint. Heavenly Father, I (we) thank You that You will renew our strength, the ones that wait upon You: that we shall mount up with wings like eagles, they we will run and not be weary we will walk and not faint. In the Name of Jesus Christ of Nazareth I (we) pray. Amen.

Ephesians 1:17-23 Prayer

Heavenly Father, I (we) pray according to Your Word, Ephesians 1:17-23, that You will give each of us a spirit of wisdom and revelation in the knowledge of Christ Jesus. I (we) pray that the eyes of our understanding will be enlightened so we may know what is the hope of the calling of Christ Jesus and the riches of the glory of Christ Jesus' inheritance in the saints, and what is the exceeding greatness of Your power towards us who believe, according to the working of Your mighty power which You used to raise Christ Jesus from the dead and seated Him at Your right hand in heavenly places, far above all principality and power and might and dominion, and every name that is named, not only in this age but also in the age which is to come. Heavenly Father, I (we) thank You that You put all things under the feet of Christ Jesus, and gave Him to be head over all things to the church, which is His body, the fullness of Him who fills all in all. To God be the Glory. Heavenly Father, open my (our) eyes that I (we) may see how great You are and how complete Your provision is for me (us). I (we) thank You that the victory the Lord Christ Jesus won for me (us) on the Cross and in His resurrection has been given to me (us) and I am (we are) seated with the Lord Christ Jesus in the heavenlies. Heavenly Father, by faith and in dependence upon You; I (we) put off the fleshly works of the old man and stand unto all the victory of the crucifixion where the Lord Christ Jesus provided cleansing from the old nature. I (we) put on myself (ourselves) the new man and I (we) stand into all the victory of the resurrection and the provisions that Christ Jesus has made for me (us). Heavenly Father, I (we) put off all forms of selfishness and put on myself (ourselves) the new nature of Jesus Christ with its love. I (we) put off all forms of fear and put the new nature of Jesus Christ with its courage. I (we) put off all forms of lust and put on the new nature with its righteousness, purity, and honesty. I am (we are) trusting You to show each of us how to accomplish this in our daily lives. In every way we stand into the victory of the ascension and glorification of the Lord Christ Jesus, whereby all principalities and powers were made subject to Christ Jesus. I (we) claim our place in Christ as victorious with Him over all the enemies of our souls. Holy Spirit, I (we) pray that You would fill us. Come into our lives, breakdown every idol and cast out every foe and continually lead us in prayer. I am (we are) thankful Heavenly Father for the expression of Your will for our daily lives that You have shown us in Your Word. By the power of the Lord Christ Jesus; I (we) claim all the will and destiny of God for each of us. I am (we are) thankful that You have blessed us with all spiritual blessings in heavenly places in Christ Jesus. I am (we are) thankful that You have begotten us unto a living hope by the resurrect ion of Christ Jesus from the dead. I am (we are) thankful that You have made provision for us so that we can be filled with the Spirit of God with love, joy, peace, with longsuffering, gentleness and goodness, with meekness, faithfulness and self-control in our lives. I (we) recognize that it is Your will for us and I (we) therefore reject and resist all the efforts of satan and his wicked spirits to rob us of the will of God. Lord Jesus, I (we) ask You to put a hedge of protection around our minds to protect us from the enemy of all accusations, distortions, insinuations and lies. I (we) claim the fullness of the will of God for our lives. In the Name of the Lord Christ Jesus, I (we) completely surrender myself (ourselves) to You Heavenly Father, as living sacrifices. We choose not to be conformed to this world. I (we) choose to be transformed by the renewing of our minds and I (we) pray that You would show us Your will and enable us to walk in Your will. In the Name of the Lord Jesus Christ of Nazareth, I (we) bind our wills to the will of God, I (we) bind our minds to the mind of Christ. To God be the Glory. Amen!

Ephesians 3:16-21 Prayer

Heavenly Father, I (we) pray according to Ephesians 3:16-21, I (we) ask You to grant each of us, myself, _____, and _____ according to the riches of Christ Jesus' glory, I (we) ask You to strengthen our inner man with might through Christ Jesus, that through faith, Christ may dwell in our hearts; that we are rooted and grounded in love, and we may be able to comprehend with all the saints what is the width and length and depth and height of Christ' love – to know the love of Christ; that we may be filled with all the fullness of You, Heavenly Father. I (we) thank You that Christ Jesus is able to do exceedingly abundantly above all that we ask or think according to the power that works in us, to Him be the glory in the church by Christ Jesus to all generations, forever and ever. Amen!

Luke 21:36 Prayer

Heavenly Father, I (we) come to You now in the Name of my (our) Lord and Savior Christ Jesus and I (we) pray for myself (ourselves) and each person I (we) prayed for today. Heavenly Father, I (we) pray that I (each of us) may be counted worthy to escape all things that will come to pass, and that I (we) may stand before the Son of man. Heavenly Father, I (we) thank You for keeping me (us) watchful and praying at all times, I (we) thank You letting us be counted worthy to escape all things that will come to pass. I (we) thank You for letting me (us) stand before the Son of Man, Jesus Christ. In Jesus Christ's Holy Name I (we) pray. Amen.

Traveling Mercies Prayer

Heavenly Father, I (we) come to You now in the Name of my (our) Lord and Savior Christ Jesus. Holy Spirit I (we) pray that You will quicken me (us) to hear my (our) Heavenly Father's Voice and lead me (us) in prayer. Heavenly Father, I (we) bow and worship before You. I (we) come to You with praise and with thanksgiving. I (we) come to You in humility, in fear, and in trembling. I (we) come to You in gratitude, in love, and through the precious Blood of Your Son Jesus Christ of Nazareth. Heavenly Father, I (we) ask You to give me and every person I prayed for today traveling mercies and to deliver us safely to our destinations. I (we) ask You to deliver us safely to our destinations. I (we) ask You to loose Your angels to go before us and to protect us and to force all darkness and all destructive forces away from us. If Your angels have to manifest themselves to protect us, please let them do so. Amen!

Psalms Warfare Prayers

Psalms 21 Prayer

O'Lord, I shall joy in Your strength, and in Your salvation how greatly shall He rejoice! You have given Him His heart's desire and have not withheld the request of His lips. For You anticipate Him with the blessings of goodness. You set a crown of pure gold on His head. He asked life of You, and You gave it to Him, even length of days forever and ever. His glory is great in Your salvation: honour and majesty have You laid upon Him. For You have made Him most blessed for ever: You have made Him exceeding glad with Your countenance. He trusts in You LORD, and through the mercy of the most High, He shall not be moved. Your hand shall find out all Your enemies: Your right hand shall find out those that hate You. You shall make them as a fiery oven in the time of Your anger: the LORD shall swallow them up in His wrath, and the fire shall devour them. Their fruit You shall destroy from the earth, and their seed from among the children of men. For they intended evil against You: they imagined a mischievous device, which they are not able to perform. Therefore You shall make them turn their back, when You shall make ready Your arrows upon Your strings against the face of them. Be exalted, LORD, in Your own strength: so we will sing and praise Your power, amen.

Psalms 31 Prayer

O' God, I come to You in both humble faith and in prayer; I come, and I lay before Your feet, my every burden and care. Hear me gracious God, my cry to You. Hear me, as I pray. Save me, and strengthen me. I know you are abiding in me each day. You O' God, are my Rock. You are my shelter and my mighty fortress; my comfort in times of sorrow; my peace in times of pain and distress. O' my God, I trust in You! On Your divine promises, I shall stand firmly; I belong to You. I know I am safe and secure in the palm of Your mighty hand.

Be my protection from the assaults and attacks from the enemy and from sin; And when my spirit grows weary, let Your Word and Spirit, revive me again. O' my God, I trust in You! I call daily upon Your blessed holy name; Let not my faith and trust in You be put to shame. Praise the Lord! I will trust in You to keep me strong; Guide me, O' Lord, and keep me from all sin and wrong thinking. O' my God, I trust in You to keep me and hold me in Your loving arms. You, Lord Jesus, look upon our souls, when we are in trouble. You search our souls, O'Lord to see if we are truly humbled by our sin and made better by our affliction. I trust You, Lord Jesus, to bring us through every danger and deliverance until we are delivered from death, our last enemy. In Jesus Name I pray. In God Be the Glory. Amen.

Psalms 32 Prayer

Heavenly Father, I (we) come to You now in the Name of my (our) Lord and Savior Christ Jesus. Heavenly Father, I (we) pray for myself (ourselves) and everyone that I (we) prayed for today and I (we) ask You to bless me (us). I (we) ask You to forgive my (our) transgression and cover my (our) sin. I (we) ask that I (we) are blessed as to the man unto whom the LORD imputeth not iniquity and in whose spirit there is no guile. When I (we) kept silence, my (our) bones waxed old through my (our) groaning all the day long. For day and night thy hand was heavy upon me (us): my (our) moisture is turned into the drought of summer. Selah. I (We) acknowledged my (our) sin unto thee, and my (our) iniquity I (we) have not hid. I (We) ask that I (we) may confess our transgressions unto the LORD; and I (we) ask that You may forgive the iniquity of my (our) sin. Selah. For this shall every one that is godly pray unto thee in a time when thou mayest be found: surely in the floods of great waters they shall not come nigh unto him. I (we) ask that You are my (our) hiding place; thou shalt preserve me (us) from trouble; You shalt compass me (us) about with songs of deliverance. Selah. I (we) ask that You will instruct me (us) and teach me (us) in the way which I (we) shalt go: I (we) ask that You will guide me (us) with Your eye. I (we) ask that I (we) will not be as the horse, or as the mule, which have no understanding: whose mouth must be held in with bit and bridle, lest they come near unto You. Many sorrows shall be to the wicked: but he that trusteth in the LORD, mercy shall compass us about. I (we) ask that I (we) be glad in the LORD, and rejoice, and be righteous: and I (we) may shout for joy, and be upright in heart. Heavenly Father, I (we) thank You that I (we) are blessed and my (our) transgression is forgiven, that my (our) sin is covered. That I (we) are blessed as to the man unto whom the LORD imputeth not iniquity and in whose spirit there is no guile. When I (we) kept silence, our bones waxed old through my (our) groaning all the day long. For day and night thy hand was heavy upon me (us): my (our) moisture is turned into the drought of summer. Selah. I (we) thank You that we acknowledged my (our) sin unto thee, and my (our) iniquity I (we) have not hid. I (we) thank You that I (we) may confess my (our) transgressions unto the LORD; and I (we) thank you that You may forgive the iniquity of my (our) sin. Selah. I (we) thank You that I (we) shall, everyone that is godly, pray unto thee in a time when thou mayest be found: surely in the floods of great waters they shall not come nigh unto him. I (we) thank You that You are my (our) hiding place; thou shalt preserve me (us) from trouble; You shalt compass me (us) about with songs of deliverance. Selah. I (we) thank You that You will instruct me (us) and teach me (us) in the way which I (we) shalt go: I (we) thank You that You will guide me (us) with Your eye. I (we) thank You that I (we) will not be as the horse, or as the mule, which have no understanding: whose mouth must be held in with bit and bridle, lest they come near unto You. Many sorrows shall be to the wicked: but he that trusteth in the LORD, mercy shall compass me (us) about. I (We) ask that I (we) be glad in the LORD, and rejoice, and be righteous: and I (we) may shout for joy, and be upright in heart. In the Name of Jesus Christ of Nazareth I (we) pray. Amen.

Psalms 35 Prayer

Heavenly Father, I (we) come to You now in the Name of my (our) Lord and Savior Christ Jesus. Heavenly Father, I (we) pray for myself and everyone that I (we) prayed for today and I (we) ask that You will plead my (our) cause, a LORD, with them that strive with me (us). I (we) ask You to fight against them that fight against me (us). Lord, I (we) ask that You take hold of shield and buckler, and stand up for my (our) help. I (we) ask You to draw out the spear, and stop them that persecute me (us): I (we) ask You to say unto my (our) souls, I (we) am your salvation. I (we) ask that they be confounded and put to shame that seek after my (our) souls: let them be turned back and brought to confusion that devises my (our) hurt. Let them be as chaff before the wind: and let the angel of the LORD chase them. Let their way be dark and slippery: and let the angel of the LORD persecute them. For without cause have they hid for me (us) their net in a pit, which without cause they have dug for our souls. I (we) ask that destruction come upon him at unawares; and let this net that he hath hid; catch himself: into that very destruction let him fall. I (we) ask that my (our) souls shall be joyful in the LORD. I (we) ask that we shall rejoice in our salvation. I (we) ask that all of my (our) bones shall say, LORD, who is like unto thee, which delivers the poor from him that is too strong for him. Amen!

Prayer for Those Who Remember and Bless the Poor (Psalms 41)

Heavenly Father, I (we) know that Your Word is true and that Your Word does not return to You void. Heavenly Father it is written in Psalms 41 that You will bless those who have considered and blessed the poor, and You will deliver each of us in our times of trouble, and that You will preserve us and keep us alive and that we will be blessed on the earth because we do remember and bless the poor. Heavenly Father it is written in Psalms 41 that You will not deliver us to the will of our enemies and that You will heal us and strengthen us on our sickbeds because we do remember and bless the poor, Heavenly Father we each ask You for mercy and to heal our souls. Lord Jesus, we know that even though our enemies speak evil words, lies, declarations, decrees, place curses on us and even praying witchcraft prayers over us, that You will break and destroy all words, declarations, decrees, and curses. We ask You to destroy any demonic attacks, assaults, curses, and witchcraft curses coming against us. In the Name of Jesus Christ, we ask You, Lord Jesus, to not allow our enemies to attack us or prevail against us because we do remember and bless the poor. Lord Jesus, we ask You to be merciful to us O'Lord and raise us up, and we thank You Lord Jesus that no attacks or any of these things will triumph over us because we remember and bless the poor. We ask You Lord Jesus, to do all these things according to Your Word in John 14:14, and we know Your Word is True. As for me (us) we ask You to uphold us in our integrity and set us before Your face forever. Bless be the Lord God of Israel from everlasting, to everlasting. To God be the Glory. Amen

Psalms 51 Prayer

Heavenly Father have mercy on me/us, our children and grandchildren, our friends and family and the people we have prayed for and according to Your loving kindness, and according to the multitude of Your tender mercies blot out all our transgressions, and wash us totally from our iniquities and cleanse us from our sins. For we do acknowledge our transgressions and our sin is always before us, and against You and You only have we sinned and have done this evil in Your sight. That You may be found just when You speak and blameless when You judge. Behold we were brought forth in iniquity and in sin our mother conceived us, and behold You desire truth in the inward parts, in the hidden parts You will make us to know wisdom. Purge us with hyssop, we shall be clean, wash us and we shall be whiter than snow. Make us to know Your joy and gladness that the bones that You have broken may rejoice and hide Your face from our sins, and blot out our iniquities. Create in us a clean heart O'God and renew a stedfast spirit within us and do not cast us away from Your Presence. Please do not take Your Holy Spirit from us but restore to us the joy of Your salvation and uphold us by Your generous Spirit that we would be able to teach transgressors Your ways and sinners can be converted to You. Deliver us from the bed of affliction O'God, the God of our salvation and our tongue shall sing aloud of Your Righteousness. O'Lord open our lips and our mouths shall show forth Your praise. For You did not desire sacrifice or else we would give it, and You do not delight in burnt offerings, the sacrifices of God are a humble spirit, a broken and contrite heart. These O'God You will not despise, do good in Your good pleasure to Zion. Amen.

Psalms 61 Prayer

Heavenly Father, I (we) come to You now in the Name of my (our) Lord and Savior Christ Jesus. Heavenly Father, I (we) pray for myself (ourselves) and everyone that I (we) prayed for today and I (we) ask that You will hear my (our) cry, O God; attend unto my (our) prayers. From the end of the earth will I (we) cry unto thee, when my (our) hearts are overwhelmed; lead me (us) to the rock that is higher than me (us). For thou hast been a shelter for me (us) and a strong tower from the enemy. I (We) ask that I (we) can abide in thy tabernacle for ever: I (we) ask that I (we) can trust in the shelter of thy wings. For thou, O God, I (we) ask that You hear my (our) vows: You hast given me (us) the heritage of those that fear Your Name. I (we) ask that You will prolong the king's life: and his years as many generations. I (We) ask that he shall abide before God forever: prepare mercy and truth, which may preserve him. So will I (we) sing praise unto Your Name forever, that I (we) may daily perform my (our) vows. Heavenly Father, I (we) thank You that You will hear my (our) cry and attend unto my (our) prayers. I (we) thank You that from the end of the earth will I (we) cry unto thee, when our hearts are overwhelmed; I (we) thank You for leading us to the rock that is higher than me (us). I (We) thank You for being a shelter for me (us), and a strong tower from the enemy. I (we) thank You for me (us) abiding in thy tabernacle for ever: that I (we) trust in the cover of thy wings. O God, I (we) thank You that You hear my (our) vows: I (we) thank You for giving me (us) the heritage of those that fear Your Name. I (we) thank You that You will prolong the king's life and his years as many generations. I (we) thank You that he shall abide before God for ever. Thank You for preparing mercy and truth; that will preserve me (us). I (we) thank You that I (we) sing praise unto Your Name forever, that I (we) daily perform my (our) vows. In the Name of Jesus Christ of Nazareth I (we) pray. Amen.

Psalms 64 Prayer

Heavenly Father, I (we) come to You now in the Name of my (our) Lord and Savior Christ Jesus. Heavenly Father, I (we) pray for myself (ourselves) and everyone that I (we) prayed for today. I (we) ask You to hear my (our) voice in my meditation and preserve my (our) life from fear of the enemy. God, I (we) ask You to hide me (us) from the secret counsel of the wicked; from the rebellion of the workers of iniquity: Who whet their tongue like a sword, and bend their bows to shoot their arrows, even bitter words: That they may shoot in secret at the perfect: suddenly they shoot at him, and do fear not. They encourage themselves in an evil matter: they commune of laying snares privily; they say, Who shall see them? They search out iniquities: they accomplish a diligent search: both the inward thought of every one of them, and the heart, is deep. But God shall shoot at them with an arrow; suddenly shall they be wounded. So they shall make their own tongue to fall upon themselves: all that see them shall fall away. All men shall fear, and shall declare the work of God; for they shall wisely consider His doing. The righteous shall be glad in the LORD, and shall trust in him; and all the upright in heart shall glory. Amen!

Psalm 67 Prayer

We know Lord that all my (our) happiness comes from Your mercy; so I (we) pray that You Lord, be merciful to me (us). I ask

You, Lord, to continue to cause Your face to shine upon me (us). Pardon me (us) from all my (our) sins. God, I (we) need your grace and blessings. Everything that I (we) have, everything that I (we) need, comes from you and you alone. Most of all, I (we) need you. I (we) need to know you. I (we) need to have the light of your face shine on me (us), so Father, show grace to me (us). Bless me (us) abundantly. But also help me (us) to remember that you give your blessings not just for me (us) alone, but that I (we) might be a blessing for others. You show me (us) your ways that I (we) might humbly teach your way to others. You save my (our) life (ives) now and for eternity that I (we) might give my (our) life (ives) for the salvation of others. Father, help me (us) to not look so intently on gifts you have given me (us) that I (we) no longer seek your face. Help me (us) to not cling to my (our) blessings so tightly that I (we) can't open my (our) hands to give to others or even to receive more from you. Help me (us) not to fear that if I (we) give, you won't be able to replenish what I (we) lack. Help me (us) to trust your sufficiency, your abundance even, and that whatever is for your glory is ultimately for my (our) good–no matter what the initial cost. In Jesus Name We Pray. Amen.

Psalms 103 Prayer

Heavenly Father we come to you now and we enter Your Gates with thanksgiving, we enter Your Courts with praise Father, we give You Glory Father, we give You Honor, we bless Your Holy Name. Bless the Lord oh my soul, and forget not all His benefits, bless the Lord oh my soul and all that is within me. Bless His Holy Name! For He's our Lord Who forgives us of all our sins, Who heals us of all our diseases, who redeems our lives from destruction and who crowns us with loving kindness and tender mercies and satisfies our mouths with good things. We thank You for Your Word Heavenly Father. We thank You that Your Word says in Psalms 103 that You will renew our youth like the eagles and execute righteousness and justice for all who are oppressed. That You give Your angels charge over us. We thank You Lord for giving us mercy, for those who fear You and that Your mercy is everlasting to everlasting. We thank You Lord for removing all our transgressions. We bless the Lord and all His works, in all places of His dominion. Bless the Lord, O my soul. In Jesus Name I pray and to God be the Glory. Amen

Touching God's Anointed (Psalms 105:15 & 1 Samuel 26:10)

Dear Heavenly Father, I come to you with praise and Thanksgiving. I humble myself before you as your anointed child. I plead my cause, O'Lord, with those that strive against me. Draw out also the spear, and stop the way against them that persecute me. Let them be turned back and brought to confusion that devise my hurt. Let them be chaff before the wind and let the angel of the Lord chase them from my presence. They have become false witnesses and have raised up against me charging me with things that I have not done. Lord, I ask you to send your ministering angels and ask you to place your hedge of protection around me to protect me from my enemies according to Job 1:10. Lord how long will you look on and do nothing. You have declared in Psalm 105:15 that no one is to touch your anointed and do them any harm. Lord I am declaring now as an anointed child of God that no one can touch me according to I Samuel 26:10. In Jesus Name I Pray and to God be the Glory. Amen

Psalms 107:20 Prayer

Heavenly Father, I (we) come to You now in the Name of my (our) Lord and Savior Christ Jesus. Heavenly Father, I (we) pray for myself and everyone that I (we) prayed for today and I ask that You will send forth Your Word to heal us. I ask You to deliver us from our destruction. Heavenly Father, I (we) thank You for sending Your Word forth to heal us. I (we) thank You for healing us. I (we) thank You for delivering us from our destruction. In the Name of Jesus Christ of Nazareth I pray. Amen.

Jabez Prayer

Heavenly Father, I (we) call on You the God of Israel saying "Oh, that You would bless me (us) indeed, and enlarge my (our) territory, that Your hand would be with me (us), and that You would keep me (us) from evil, and that I (we) may not cause pain!" Father God, I (we) ask You to grant me (us) what I (we) have requested the way You did for Jabez, according to 1 Chronicles 4:9-10.

Bind My Mind to the Will of God

Heavenly Father, I (we) come to You now in the Name of my (our) Lord and Savior Christ Jesus. I (We) bind my (our) mind to the will of God, I (we) bind _____'s mind to the will of God in the Name of Jesus Christ of Nazareth. Amen!

Romans 12 Prayer

Heavenly Father, we thank You Lord for the mercies by which You allow us to present our bodies as living sacrifice, holy and acceptable, which is our spiritual service of worship to You. Dear Lord, it is not our will to be conformed to this world, but to be transformed by the renewing of our minds, that we may prove good, acceptable, and perfect to what Your will is. By grace given to us, show us how to not esteem ourselves more or less important to the body of Christ than another. Thank You Lord for the spiritual gifts that have been given to us that we may prophesy in proportion to our faith and to teach according to Your precious Word and to exhort and to give liberally and lead with diligence and show mercy with cheerfulness. Lord, show us how our love can be without hypocrisy. Teach us to abhor what is evil and cling to what is good. Teach us to be kind and affectionate to one another in honor and give preference to one another not lagging in diligence to be fervent in spirit to serve You Lord. Dear Father, we rejoice in hope, we are patient through tribulation, and we shall continue in distributing to the needs of the saints and be truly given to hospitality. We will bless those who curse and persecute us. We will rejoice with those who rejoice, and weep with those who weep. We will be of the same mind toward one another and not set our minds on high things but associate ourselves with the humble. We will not be wise in our own opinions and we will not repay anyone evil for evil for Your Word says to repay evil with good. We will not give place to wrath but will wait on the Lord for vengeance is Yours, therefore, we will live peacefully with all people and be overcomers through Christ. Lord we will offer drink to a thirsty enemy and food to one that is hungry that we may abide in Your Word forever, because we love You Heavenly Father, in Christ Jesus Holy Name we pray, with thanksgiving. Amen.

Sin List

abandonment, abduction, abhorrence of holy things, abhorring judgment, abomination, abortion, abusiveness, accusation, adulterous lust, adultery, afflicting others, aggravation, agitation, aiding and abetting sin, alcoholism, all unrighteousness, anger, animosity, anxiety, apprehension, argumentativeness, arrogance, assaults, astrology, atheism, avariciousness, Baal worship, backbiting, backsliding, bad attitude, bad language, bearing false witness, big talk, being a workaholic, being too quick to speak, believing the lies of the enemy, belittling, bereavement, betraying Jesus, bickering, bigotry, bitterness, black magic, blackmail, blasphemy, blasphemy of the Holy Spirit, boastfulness, boisterousness, bowing down to gods or serving images, bragging, brainwashing, breaking commandments of God, breaking vows and covenants to God, breaking covenants and vows with others, bribery, brutality, burning incense to gods, calamity, carelessness, cares & riches of this world, carnality, casting God away, causing disagreements, causing distress, causing division, causing fear, causing men to err, causing offense, causing poor to fail, changing truth to lies, chanting of charms, cheating, coming against God's anointed, committing willful and/or intentional sin, complaining, complacency against God's will or destiny, conceit, concupiscence, condemnation, condemning the just, causing conflict, confrontation, confusion, conjuration, conspiring against God, consulting wizards and psychics, contempt, contention, controlling, conniving, compulsiveness, contentiousness, contesting and withstanding or resisting God, corruption, counterfeiting Christian work, covering sin, coveting neighbor's spouse, spouse, brother, sister, house, land, automobile, or anything that is our neighbor's; covetousness, cravenness, criticalness, crookedness, cruelty, using crystals, cursing God, cursing, cynicalism, dealing treacherously, deceit, deception, defamation, defeatism, defiantness, defiling, degrading, dejection, *demon* consciousness, demon worship, denying Jesus and His resurrect ion, dependencies, depravity, desecration of holy vessels, desires of this world, despair, despising God, His Name and His Word, despising spouse, despising neighbors, despising parents, despitefulness, despondency, destruction of the innocent, saints and holy things; deviousness, disagreements, disbelief, discord, discouragement, discrediting, disdain, disgust, dishonesty, disliking the love of good men, disobedience, disobedient to God, disorderly, disputing, disregard of God's work, disrespectfulness of God, disruptiveness, dissension, distantness, distrust, divining, divining for water with rods, divining for money, division, divorce, domineeringness, double-talking, double mindedness, doubt, dread, driving men from true worship and inheritance, drug abuse, drunkenness, duplicity, drinking blood, eating blood, eating sin offerings, eating unclean food, effeminate behavior, egotism, enchantment, enlarged imaginations, entering into ungodly soul

<<<MISSING PAGES 36-37>>>

righteousness, turning aside for money, unbelief, unbridled lust, uncleanness, uncompromising, undermining, unequally yoked to non-believers, unfairness, unfaithfulness in trust, unfaithfulness, unforgiveness, unfriendliness, ungratefulness, unholy alliances, unholy habits, unions with menstrual women, unmanly, unmercifulness, unreadiness, unrepenting, unrighteousness of laws, unrighteousness, unruliness of tongues, unsparing, un-submissiveness, unthankfulness, untruthfulness, (being) unwise, unworthiness, using tarot cards, vain imaginations, vain repetitions, vanity, vengeance, viciousness, vile affections, vile speaking, violence, vulgarity, walking after our own devices, walking for unprofitable things, walking after our own thoughts, walking after false gods, walking with heathens, walking with sinners, water witching, white magic, wickedness, willful sin, willful blindness to the truth, winking with evil intent, witchcraft, withdrawal, withholding a pledge, (being) without concern, (being) without natural affection, (being) without mercy, working iniquity, working for praise, worldliness, worrying, worshipping possessions, worshipping our works, worshipping the creation instead of the Creator, worshipping of planets, wrathfulness, wrong doing, zealousness to make others sinful, zealousness in outward show.

Demon List

abandonment, abomination, abortion, abuse, accidents, and accident prone, accusation, accuser of the brethren, aches, addictions, adultery, adulterous lust, adversity, affectation, agitation, aggravation, alcoholism, analysis, anxiety, anger, anguish, animosity, anorexia, anti-Semitism, anti-submissiveness, anxiety, apathy, apprehension, arba, argumentativeness, arrested development, arrogance, atheism, arthritis, automatic writing, Baal, backbiting, bestiality, belittling, busyness, bickering, bitterness, black magic, blasphemy, blindness, burden, boasting, brainwashing, bribes, broken spirit, chaos, cares & riches of this world, carnality, causing offense, cheating, childish/immature behavior, Christian science, chronic sickness, complaining, covetousness, cursing, condemnation, confusion, confrontation, conjuring, conceit, concupiscence, contention, continual sorrow, contradiction, control, conniving, complacency, compulsiveness, criticalness, crooked speech, cruelty, cultic art, cynicism, daydreaming, death, deception, defeatism, deafness, defiance, defilement, dejection, delusion, depression, dependencies, despair, desires of this world, despondency, destruction, dictatorial, diotrophes, disbelief, disgust, discouragement, discomfort, discontentment, disobedience, dissension, disdain, disease, distress, distrust, distraction, driving, division, divination/ diviner, domination, doorkeeper spirits, doubt, drug abuse, drug addiction, drunkenness, dread, ego, enchanting, escapism, ego, embarrassment, embezzlement, envy, escape of reality, exasperation, false burdens, false compassion, false responsibility, false teaching, false witness, fantasy, fantasy lust, fatigue, fault finding, fear, fear of rejection, fear of man, fear of disapproval, fear of failure, fear of condemnation, fear of accusation, fear of reproof, fetishes, fighting, financial failure, forgetfulness, fornication, fortune telling, fretting, frigidity, frustration, gall, generational spirits of ______, gloom, gluttony, gout, gossip, greed, grief, guilt, hardhearted, hatred, haughtiness headaches, heaviness, hopelessness, hallucinations, harlotry, horoscopes, hurt, hyperactivity, hypocrisy, idleness, idolatries of any kind, impurity, incest, infirmity, injury, impatience, inadequacy, incantation, incoherence, incubus and succubus, ineptness, indecision, independence, indifference, insomnia, intimidation, intolerance, insecurity, insanity, insensitiveness, intellectualism, intentional sin, irritation, islam, isolation, jealousy, judgmentalness, laboring, lack of knowledge, lasciviousness, legalism, lethargy, leviathan, levitation, listlessness, lofty, loneliness, lust, lust of the eye, lust of the flesh, lust of the mind, lying, madness, magicians, manipulation, masturbation, materialism, material lust, meanness, mental illness, migraine, mind control, mischief, mockery, molestation, morbidity, murder, murmuring, necromancy, nervousness, nervous habits, nicotine addiction, occultism, opposing, oppression, obsession, obstinate, orgies, Orion, pain, paranoia, passivity, pedophilia, pendulums, perfectionism, perplexity, perverse spirit, petulance, perfection, persecution, pornography, possessiveness, pouting, plague, plotting, prejudice, premonitions, presumption, pretension, pride, pride of knowledge, procrastination, provoking, puffed up, quarreling, railing, rape, rage, rebellion, rejection, religious control, restlessness, rationalization, retaliation, retardation, rheumatism, rigidity, resentment, rottenness, rudeness, ruling spirits, sadism, scorn, seduction, shame, slander, self-accusation, self-centered, self-delusion, self-confusion, self-deception, self-rejection, self-seduction, self-pity, selfishness, self-dependent, self-destruction, self-hatred, self-righteousness, self-promotion, self-condemnation, self-criticalness, self-praise, self-torture, self-willed, self-exaltation, self-importance, serpents and scorpions, sexual idolatry, sexual impurity, shame, sharp/bitter words, shield demons, shock, shyness, sciatica, sickness, sin consciousness, skepticism, sleepiness, soothsayer, spirit of chemosh, spiders, spirit of self, spirit of unbelief, stiff necked, strife, stress, stubbornness, struggling, suspicion, suicide, taking offense, tarot cards, temper, tension, tiredness, theatrics, timidity, torment, tragedies, trauma, travail, travailing womb, unbending, uncleanness, unclean spirits, unemployment, unforgiveness, undermining, unfairness, ungodly conduct, unjust gain, un-submissiveness, unwilling to admit wrong, unwilling to apologize, unwilling to change, unyielding, unworthiness, vagabonds, vanity, violence, wandering, water witching, weariness, white magic, wickedness, willful sin, withdrawal, witches, wizards, wrath, worry, wounded spirit, witchcraft, all unrighteous spirits, demon consciousness, sophistication, intellectualism and Nimrod, high mindedness, Jezebel, Ahab, spirit of Ankh, spirit of Balaam, another Jesus, Baal, Balaam, Cora, Herodian, Python, spirit of Rachel, spirit of Saul, religion, sorcery, witch(witchcraft), voodoo, cults, occultism. All hindering, persecuting, accusing, lying, familiar spirits, seducing spirits, mind binding, mind blocking spirits, anti-christ spirits, generational spirits, all spirits and strongmen of all mental, physical, and emotional illness, sickness, diseases, disorders, death, premature death, infirmities, afflictions, inflammations, viruses, infections, abnormal cells, radical cells, lesions, cysts, pain, shock, trauma, spasms, cramps, abnormal growths, radical growths in or on any parts of our bodies including our eyes, ears, nose, mouth, throat, back, bones, muscles, ligaments, tissues, blood, blood vessels, arteries, colons, intestines, stomach, prostate, thyroid, brains, liver, pancreas, heart, lungs, cardiovascular disorders and diseases, reproductive disorders and diseases, thyroid disorders and diseases, blood pressure disorders and diseases, throat disorders and diseases, breast disorders and diseases, neurological disorders and diseases, lymphatic disorders and diseases, chemical imbalances, hormone imbalances, allergies of any kind, senility, forgetfulness, paranoia, schizophrenia; all spirits of arthritis, crippling arthritis, acute arthritis, sinusitis, acute sinusitis, sciatica, bursitis, tendonitis, discomfort, headaches, migraines, aches, pains, performance spirits; all spirits of disorders and diseases, hypoglycemia of all forms, degenerative diseases of all kinds, all cancers, all tumors, all mind diseases and disorders.

Prayer Manual

Heavenly Father, I come to You now in the Name of my Lord and Savior Christ Jesus. Holy Spirit I pray that You will quicken me to hear my Heavenly Father's Voice and lead me in prayer. Heavenly Father, I bow and worship before You. I come to You with praise and with thanksgiving. I come to You in humility, in fear, and in trembling and seeking truth. I come to You in gratitude, in love, and through the precious Blood of Your Son Jesus Christ of Nazareth. (Note—if two or more praying: Heavenly Father, ______ and I come to You in one accord in the Name of Christ Jesus of Nazareth according to Matthew 18:19)

Learning to Know His Voice

Many Christian believers do not believe that they can or do hear God's Voice. Many years ago I was reading John 10 and Jesus said in verse 14, that He is the Good Shepherd and that He knows His sheep and His sheep know Him. In John 10:27 Jesus said My sheep hear My Voice and I know them and they follow Me. I'm one of the Lord Jesus' sheep and I know that He is not a respecter of persons so I decided I wanted to hear His Voice like some of His other sheep do. I wanted to hear His Voice so He could guide me according to Isaiah 58:11 and instruct me, and teach me in the way that I should go according to Psalms 32:8. I believe that if you want to hear God's Voice and if you pray the following prayer, He will honor your prayer and teach you to hear His Voice. I remember the first time I heard His Voice and it changed my life.

Hearing God's Voice Prayer

Heavenly Father, I (we) come to You now in the Name of my (our) Lord and Savior Christ Jesus. Heavenly Father, It is written in Your Word according to John chapter 10 that Your sheep know Your Voice. Heavenly Father, I am (we are) one of Your sheep. I (we) ask You Heavenly Father, to teach me (us) to hear Your Voice distinctly and clearly according to John chapter 10. I (we) ask You increase Your anointing on me (us) to clearly hear and know Your Voice and not that of a stranger, I (we) ask You to do this in the Name of Jesus Christ of Nazareth. Give me (us) the ability Heavenly Father to hear Your Voice, I (we) ask this according to John 16:23 in the Name of Jesus Christ of Nazareth. Amen!

Testing the Spirits

Heavenly Father, it is written in Your Word in 1st John 4:1-2 that we should not believe every spirit but test the spirits to determine whether the spirits are of God. By this I will know the Spirit of God: for every spirit that confesses that Jesus Christ has come in the flesh is of God. Heavenly Father if You told me, "___________", confess, "Jesus Christ has come in the flesh." Amen. (Explanation: If you believe the Lord has told you something, the Word tells you to *test the spirits.* If the Lord does not tell you that *"Jesus Christ has come in the flesh"*, then you have not heard the Spirit of God.)

Remove Any Deception

Heavenly Father, I (we) come to You through the Precious Blood of my (our) Lord and Savior Jesus Christ, I (we) ask You to destroy and remove any deception in my (our) mind(s) in Jesus Christ's Holy Name, amen.

Confirmation by Two or Three Witnesses

In 2nd Corinthians 13:1b, there exists a very important prayer principle about confirming to us when we have heard God's Voice. The verse reads, *"By the mouth of two or three witnesses every word shall be established."* This works in the natural on establishing a testimony over certain matters (Deuteronomy 19:15) and you will find out that it works the same in the spiritual (2nd Corinthians 13:1b). We have learned that the Lord is consistent and does not tell one person one thing and then tell another person something else. For example, "Lord, did you tell brother Joe that we are to go to his friend and lay hands on him?" If I pray or you pray and get a "No" and you have made sure you are clean of sin, demonic spirits, no evil spirits in the room, you have *tested the spirits (See Testing the Spirits Prayer),* that your mind is not deceiving you, then let your friend Joe know that you heard the Lord tell you know "No." Something is going on. Maybe, it is a no, not now. Maybe it's a no, it is not necessary. Maybe Joe Has an evil spirit in HIS presence and is not hearing properly. Maybe Joe has it in his emotions or head, "well it has to be God's will!" Let the Word from the Lord to You be *established by the mouth of two or three witnesses!* Something is going on, seek God, He will reveal it to you!

Praying God's Promises For the Tither (Malachi 3)

Heavenly Father I (we) come to You now in the Name of my (our) Lord and Savior Jesus Christ of Nazareth and Heavenly Father as I (we) pay my (our) tithes according to Your Word in Malachi 3, I (we) claim and ask You to fulfill the seven promises that You have given to me (us) as a tither'(s). Heavenly Father You know that I (we) tithe and I (we) ask You to revive us because I (we) have obeyed You by paying our tithe according Malachi 3:10. Heavenly Father, You have promised me (us) according to Your Word that because I (we) pay You our tithes that You will open the Windows of Heaven and pour out a blessing on me (us) that there shall not be enough room to receive it. Heavenly Father You have promised me (us) in Malachi 3 that because of my (our) tithe(s) that I (we) will be prosperous. Heavenly Father it says in Your Word in Malachi 3:11, that You will rebuke the devourer for me (us). So I (we) ask You Lord to rebuke the devourer for my (our) sakes because of my (our) obedience to You in paying my (our) tithe(s). Heavenly Father Your Word says that You promise to cripple and paralyze the enemy so he will not be able to come near me (us). Heavenly Father I (we) ask You not to let the enemy destroy the fruits of my (our) ground according to Malachi 3:11. Heavenly Father I (we) ask You to prevent the enemy from touching my (our) finances, the fruits of my (our) ground, because of my (our) obedience to You in paying my (our) tithe(s). Heavenly Father I (we) ask You that my (our) vine not cast it's fruit before it's time; according to Your Word in Malachi 3. Heavenly Father, I (we) ask You to stop the enemy from touching and from coming near me or any member of my (our) families, finances, fruits, and ground, because we are obedient to You in paying our tithes. Heavenly Father I (we) ask You to keep our families, our finances, our fruits, and our grounds, bless me (us) with Your seven blessings of the tither, as written in Malachi 3. I (we) ask You to give us fulfillment of these 7 blessings of a thither according to John 16:23. Father we have been obedient in paying our tithe and we receive the blessing. Father cause all the nations to call us blessed because we are tithers, in Jesus Christ's Holy Name and to God be the Glory. Amen.

The Prayer For Judges

Heavenly Father, I (we) ask You to forgive Judge ________ for any un-forgiveness, for all of his/her sins, iniquities, trespasses, transgressions, sins of commission, sins of omission and any unknown sins according to Psalms 19:12.

According to Your Word in Matthew 16:19, I (we) have been given the Keys to Your Kingdom of Heaven and whatever I (we) bind and loose on earth shall be bound and loosed in heaven. So I (we) ask You to loose Your angels in great abundance into Judge ________'s presence, the presence of his/her courtrooms, into their rooms, their chambers, halls, restrooms, and work areas.

Now I (we) bind, in the Name of Jesus Christ, all of satan's evil wicked demons, lying and tormenting spirits and strongmen along with all their works, roots, fruits, tentacles and links; along with all evil principalities, powers, and rulers of wickedness in high places and command them not to manifest and transfer into Judge ________'s presence. I bind and command them not to manifest themselves or transfer themselves onto anybody's presence in Judge ______'s courtroom.

Heavenly Father, it is written in Psalms 91 and Matthew 6 in Your Word that You are our deliverer and I (we) ask that You give Judge _____ and every organ, every gland, every cell in his/her body—total deliverance, total freedom, total liberty and total salvation from all evil, foul, wicked, demon, lying, perverse, unclean, foul, demonic spirits, strongmen, and his/her messengers, and from all sicknesses, diseases, infirmities, afflictions, infections, viruses, inflammations, disorders of any kind in every cell in their body, in every gland in their body, in every organ in his/her body; rooms, chambers, court rooms, halls, restrooms, and work areas, and wherever they are at this time. I (we) thank You for giving Judge _____ this deliverance, freedom, liberty and salvation from all these things in the Name of the Lord Jesus Christ of Nazareth according to John 16:23. May these deliverances be used to glorify You, Heavenly Father.

I (we) apply the Blood of Jesus over, under, and around every attorney, policeman, law official, all the Court House staff and anyone else that comes into their presence, the airways that surround them, their rooms, their chambers, court rooms, halls, restrooms, and work areas, every place that Judge ______ may be; and anybody that Judge ______ comes in contact with today and everyday. I (we) ask You to render powerless and harmless and nullify, destroy, and cancel the power of any evil spirit, demonic spirit, demonic strongman, messenger of satan that tries to come into their presence or anyone that is around Judge ______ in the Name of Jesus Christ of Nazareth.

Heavenly Father, I (we) ask You to fill Judge ______ with Your precious Holy Spirit. I (we) ask You to fill Judge ______ with all of Your fruits of Your Holy Spirit including Your love, Your joy, Your peace, Your gentleness, Your goodness, Your meekness, Your faithfulness and Your self-control.

Heavenly Father, in Christ Jesus Holy Name; I (we) ask You to fill Judge ______ with Your Holy Ghost anointing and power, cover them with Your presence, Your anointing and Your power in the Name of Jesus Christ of Nazareth.

Loose extra angels around Judge ______ and leave them there as long as Judge ______ is in the Court House, to guard and protect him/her. In Jesus Name I (we) pray. To God be the Glory. Amen!

Pastor's Prayer

Heavenly Father, I come to You in the Name of my Lord and Savior, Jesus Christ. I come to You with praise and thanksgiving, in worship, in humbleness and through the Blood of my Lord and Savior, Jesus Christ of Nazareth. Holy Spirit I ask You to quicken me to my Heavenly Father's Voice and reveal to me all un-confessed sins I have in my heart at this time. I ask You to forgive me of any sins of ______, ______, ______ and ______, and any hidden or unknown sins according to Psalms 19:12. Heavenly Father, I ask you to forgive me and ______, ______, ______, & ______, and Pastor ______________, for any un-forgiveness, the leadership, the intercessors and all of the families attending __________ Church for all of our sins and cleanse us from all unrighteousness, according to 1 John 1:9. Your Word says in 1 John 1:9 that if we confess our sins that you are faithful and just to forgive us and cleanse us of all unrighteousness. Heavenly Father Your Word says in Matthew 6:15 that if I don't forgive others You won't forgive me, so, I forgive ______ & ______ for anything they have ever said or done to me and I bless them in the Name of Jesus Christ and I ask You to forgive them and bless them in the Name of the Lord Jesus Christ. Heavenly Father, I ask you to cover all of our sins, iniquities, trespasses and transgressions with the Blood of Jesus Christ. Lord Jesus, I ask You to destroy any ungodly prayers, witchcraft prayers, psychic prayers, or evil words, side effects, effects, and influences that have been prayed or spoken over me or anyone that I pray for today. I ask You to destroy any assignments or plans that satan has against us, our children, grandchildren, businesses, finances, ministries, cars, homes, or properties. I ask You to cause Your anointing to break and destroy the yokes of all bondages that are over us along with all their works. Lord Jesus, I ask You to pull down and destroy and cast aside all demonic strongholds, vain imaginations, and any high thoughts in each of us that exalts itself against the knowledge of God, and to bring every thought captive in each of us to the obedience of Christ according to 2 Corinthians 10:3-6. I thank You that no weapon formed against us shall prosper. Lord Jesus I ask You to do all these things according to John 14:14, to God be the glory. Heavenly Father, it is written in Psalms 91 and Matthew 6 and many other places that You are our Deliverer, and I ask You to give me and every person that I pray for today total deliverance, total freedom, total liberty, total salvation, from all sickness, diseases, infirmities, afflictions, infections, viruses, abnormal cells, radical cells and I ask You to give us this according to John 16:23. Heavenly Father, I plead the Blood of Jesus Christ over me and everybody I pray for today, our houses, cars, offices, properties, buildings, and ask You to render powerless and harmless, and to destroy any demonic spirit, strongman, curses, witchcraft prayers, psychic prayers, destructive forces that try to come against us. Heavenly Father, I ask You to fill me and each person I pray for today with Your Holy Spirit and all the fruits of Your Holy Spirit. Heavenly Father, I submit my life to You and I trust You and love You, with all my heart, soul, mind and strength. I bind each of our wills to the will of God and each of our minds to the mind of Christ. Heavenly Father, I ask You to put a hedge of protection around us to protect us from the enemy. Heavenly Father, I apply the full armor of God over me and everyone I pray for today. According to Ephesians 6, Heavenly Father, help us to know and hear your Voice and to walk in righteousness. Lord Jesus I ask You to fulfill Your will and destiny for each of our lives, help each to respond to the conviction of Your Holy Spirit. Heavenly Father, please help us to keep our eyes fixed and focused on our Lord Jesus Christ. Heavenly Father, I ask you to Bless me and everyone that I pray for today, guard us and protect us and let your Holy Spirit comfort us, guide us, convict us and lead us into all truth. We choose health and wholeness today in Christ Jesus and through Him we are victorious. Heavenly Father, I ask you to release your healing virtue into each of our bodies and to give each of us divine health. Heavenly Father, we ask You to give us all these things according to John 16:23. Lord Jesus we ask You to help us walk in your perfect love, presence, and anointing that God may be glorified in Jesus Name, according to John 14:14, to God be the Glory. Amen!

Hospital Prayer

Heavenly Father, I (we) ask You to forgive (________) for any un-forgiveness, for all of his/her sins, iniquities, trespasses, transgressions, sins of commission, sins of omission and specifically any sins of ______, ______, or ______; and any unknown sins according to Psalms 19:12.

According to Your Word in Matthew 16:19, I (we) have been given the Keys to the Kingdom of Heaven and whatever I (we) bind and loose on earth shall be bound and loosed in heaven. So I (we) ask You to loose Your angels in great abundance into (_______s) presence, the presence of every doctor, every nurse, into his/her room, the surgery unit, and recovery room. Now I (we) bind, in the Name of Jesus Christ, all of satan's evil wicked demons, lying and tormenting spirits and strongmen along with all their works, roots, fruits, tentacles and links; along with all evil principalities, powers, and rulers of wickedness in high places and command them not to manifest and transfer into ('s) presence, nor the doctors' or nurses' presence, or into (________'s) room, surgery unit, recovery room, and every place that (________) may be. Heavenly Father, it is written in Psalms 91 and Matthew 6 in Your Word that You are our Deliverer and I (we) ask that You give (______) every organ, every gland, every cell, every bone, every muscle, every ligament, in his/her body—total deliverance, total freedom, total liberty and total salvation from all evil, wicked, demon, lying, perverse, unclean, foul, demonic spirits, strongmen, and their messengers, and from all sicknesses, diseases, destructive organisms, bacteria, MRSA, viruses, and fungi, infirmities, afflictions, infections, inflammations, abnormal cells, radical cells, abnormal growths, radical growths, all cancers, tumors, and disorders of any kind in every cell, every gland, every organ in his/her body. In his/her room and wherever they are at this time. I (we) thank You for giving (______) this deliverance, freedom, liberty and salvation from all these things in the Name of the Lord Jesus Christ of Nazareth according to John 16:23. Heavenly Father, I (we) ask You to release Your miracle virtue, Your Healing virtue into (______) in the Name of the Lord Jesus Christ of Nazareth. Heavenly Father, I (we) plead the Blood of Jesus Christ over (______), from the top of his/her head to the soles of his/her feet, under and around every doctor, every nurse, all the hospital staff in his/her presence, the airways that surround him/her, the surgery unit, recovery room, every place that (______) may be; and anybody that (______) comes in contact with today and every day. I (we) ask You to render powerless and harmless and nullify, destroy, and cancel the power of any evil spirit, demonic spirit, demonic strongman, messenger of satan that tries to come into his/her presence or anyone that is around me (______) in the Name of Jesus Christ of Nazareth. Heavenly Father, I (we) ask You to fill (______) with Your precious Holy Spirit. I (we) ask You to fill (______) with the fruits of Your Holy Spirit including Your love, Your joy, Your peace, Your gentleness, Your goodness, Your meekness, Your faithfulness and Your self-control. Heavenly Father, in Christ Jesus' Holy Name; I (we) ask You to fill (______) with Your Holy Ghost anointing and power, cover him/her with Your presence, Your anointing and Your power in the Name of Jesus Christ of Nazareth.

Heavenly Father, I ask you now according to John 16:23, in the Name of our Lord and Savior Jesus Christ of Nazareth to release your miracle virtue, your miracle anointing into (__________) in the Name of Jesus Christ of Nazareth, and ask that your miracle virtue, and miracle anointing flow through every cell, every organ, every gland, every part of (______)'s body in the Name of Jesus Christ of Nazareth. I ask you to give divine healing and divine health, wholeness and newness of life according to John 16:23 in the Name of the Holy Jesus Christ of Nazareth. Heavenly Father, I ask you to let the manifestation of every miracle and every healing that you have given (__________) be manifested in him/her now in the Name of Jesus Christ of Nazareth. Heavenly Father, I ask you to loose extra angels around (__________) and leave them there as long as (__________) is in the hospital, to guard and protect him/her. In Jesus' Name we pray. To God be the Glory. Amen!

Prayer for Inmates

Heavenly Father, I ask You to forgive, ________________, their fellow inmates, their guards, their warden, and all the staff members at ________________ prison (jail) for any un-forgiveness, for all their sins, transgressions, iniquities and trespasses and to cleanse them of all unrighteousness in the Name of our Lord Jesus Christ.

I bind all of Satan's evil wicked demon, lying, tormenting, perverse, and unclean spirits that are in ________________'s presence, the presence of their cells, rooms, recreational areas, work areas, and loose them from ________________'s presence, and from the presence of these areas and any other areas that ________________ will be in today.

Heavenly Father, according to Your Word in Matthew 16 and 18, You have given me the Keys to the Kingdom of Heaven and whatever I bind and loose on earth shall be bound and loosed in heaven. I ask You to loose Your angels in great abundance into ________________'s presence; the presence of their cells, rooms, buildings, or any other areas they're in or will be in today.

Heavenly Father, it is written in Psalms 91 and Matthew 6, that You are our deliverer and I ask that You give

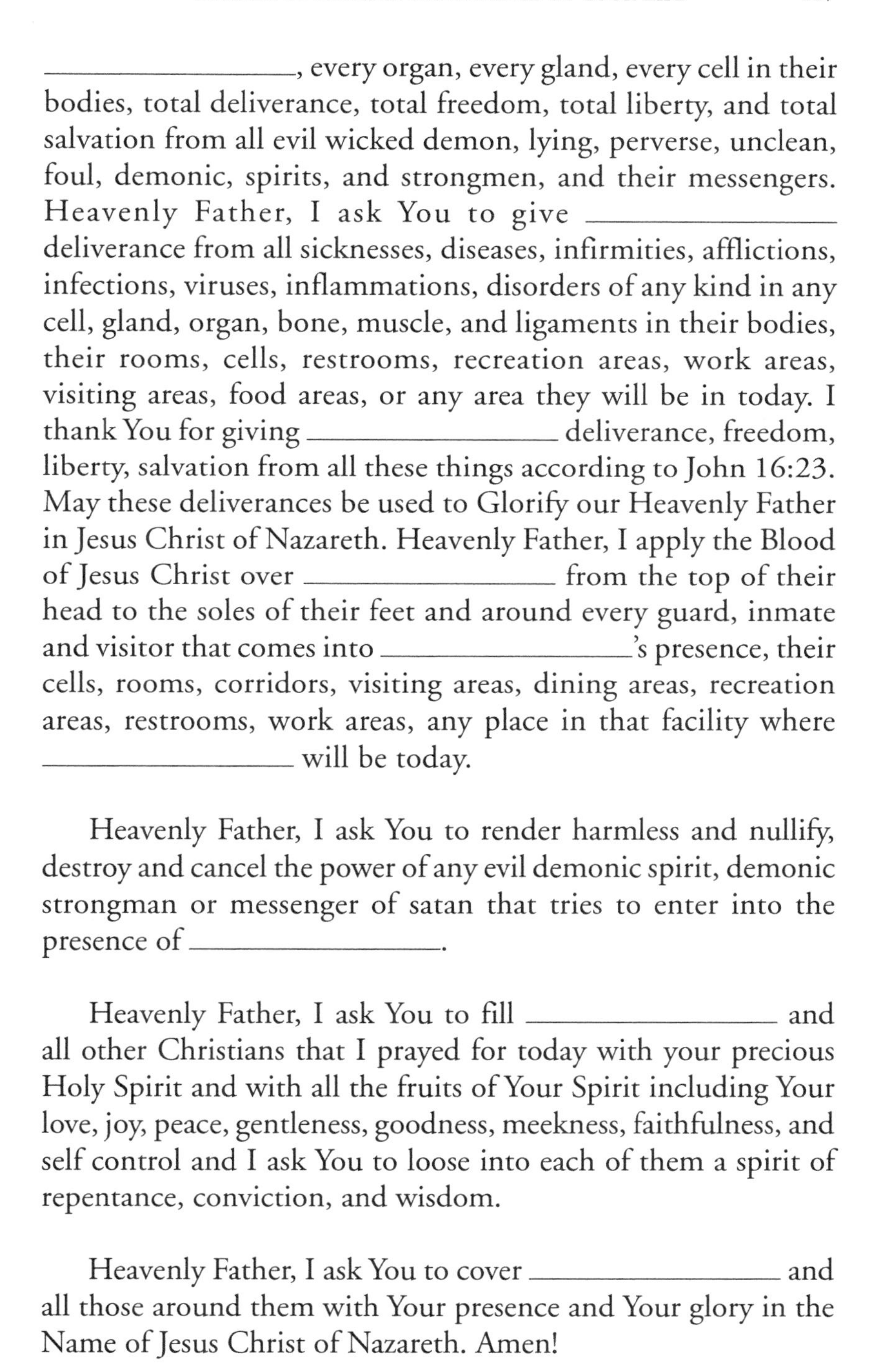

________________, every organ, every gland, every cell in their bodies, total deliverance, total freedom, total liberty, and total salvation from all evil wicked demon, lying, perverse, unclean, foul, demonic, spirits, and strongmen, and their messengers. Heavenly Father, I ask You to give ________________ deliverance from all sicknesses, diseases, infirmities, afflictions, infections, viruses, inflammations, disorders of any kind in any cell, gland, organ, bone, muscle, and ligaments in their bodies, their rooms, cells, restrooms, recreation areas, work areas, visiting areas, food areas, or any area they will be in today. I thank You for giving ________________ deliverance, freedom, liberty, salvation from all these things according to John 16:23. May these deliverances be used to Glorify our Heavenly Father in Jesus Christ of Nazareth. Heavenly Father, I apply the Blood of Jesus Christ over ________________ from the top of their head to the soles of their feet and around every guard, inmate and visitor that comes into ________________'s presence, their cells, rooms, corridors, visiting areas, dining areas, recreation areas, restrooms, work areas, any place in that facility where ________________ will be today.

Heavenly Father, I ask You to render harmless and nullify, destroy and cancel the power of any evil demonic spirit, demonic strongman or messenger of satan that tries to enter into the presence of ________________.

Heavenly Father, I ask You to fill ________________ and all other Christians that I prayed for today with your precious Holy Spirit and with all the fruits of Your Spirit including Your love, joy, peace, gentleness, goodness, meekness, faithfulness, and self control and I ask You to loose into each of them a spirit of repentance, conviction, and wisdom.

Heavenly Father, I ask You to cover ________________ and all those around them with Your presence and Your glory in the Name of Jesus Christ of Nazareth. Amen!

Law Enforcement, Emergency Medical Personnel, Firemen, and Postal Workers

Heavenly Father, I come to You in Jesus Christ's Holy Name. I ask You Lord Jesus Christ according to John 14:14 to forgive all people involved with Law Enforcement, Emergency Medical Services, Firemen, and Postal Services, of all un-forgiveness. Lord I ask You to give these people and their vehicles "traveling mercies" back and forth where ever they are today. I ask You Lord to loose Your angels around about them and any passengers, to guard, protect and minister to them. Lord Jesus, protect these people, that no harm would to come to these people who are serving us and our communities! Give them each alertness, an awakened and sharp mind, with abundant energy, and stamina to go through what they are having to face, from the time they get up, till the time they fall asleep. Prepare them mentally and physically to handle each situation as it arises. Place them on the hearts and minds of Your Intercessors and Prayer Warriors everywhere to stand in the gap and make up the hedge for their lives. I ask You Lord Jesus to shield, protect, and keep them from mental and physical injury, hurt, harm, broken limbs, bodily damage and trauma. Also protect their vehicles from other vehicles and people. Bless them in what they put their hands to do for us and the community. Renew and refresh their souls and bodies as they go, that stress, fatigue, and bad health will not have any place in their lives. Lord Jesus I ask You to destroy all wrong words, the power of all wrong words, and cause demonic spirits to flee from their paths into the Abyss bound deaf, dumb, blind and mute, and evil schemes against them totally ineffective, throughout this day and into tomorrow afternoon. Lord cause their minds to focus clearly to achieve each task set before them. Lord I (we) pray that You restore, bless, and prosper their marriages, friendships, and families relationships. That they and their loved ones come to know You, Your love, Your mercy, Your Saving Grace, and come into an intimate knowing and relationship with the One True Lord and Savior, Jesus Christ, Son of God, in all these things according to Your Sovereign will, to God be the Glory, amen!

Lord, we ask forgiveness and salvation for those they transport, whether it be someone that is hurt, a criminal, or a co-worker, we lift them before You. Lord help the injured get to the hospital in time, so they will live and receive proper life saving treatment! Heavenly Father I ask in Jesus Christ's Holy Name that these people and their loved ones will be drawn to You, and come to Your saving grace and knowledge of our Lord and Savior Jesus Christ, and an eternal relationship with You. In all these things, Lord Jesus we ask that lives will be changed through Law Enforcement, Medical Personnel, Firemen, and Postal Workers, to Your Glory, for Your Kingdom Heavenly Father, forever and ever, Your Sovereign Will be done, amen!

Prayer for a Person Who is Grieving Over the Loss of a Loved One

Please help me in this time of loss of ________________. I seem to be frozen with this overwhelming grief. I don't understand why my life is filled with this pain and heartache. But I turn my eyes to you as I seek to find the strength to trust in your faithfulness. You, Lord are a God of comfort and love and I ask You to help me to patiently wait on you and not despair; I will quietly wait for your salvation. My heart is crushed, but I know that you will not abandon me forever. Please show me your compassion, Lord. Help me through the pain so that I will hope in you again. I believe the promise in your Word to send me fresh mercy each day. Though I can't see past today, I trust your love will never fail me.

Jesus, You came to heal the brokenhearted and my heart is broken today Lord, and only you can heal my sorrow over losing ____________. I ask You, Lord to comfort me because You love me and have promised me everlasting consolation and hope through Your grace.

Blessed be to God, even the Father of our Lord Jesus Christ, the Father of mercies, and the God of all comfort; Who comforts me in all my tribulations, that I may be protected from any trouble and hurt as I walk with You, Lord, through the grief of losing ______________.

In Jesus Name I pray. Amen

Comprehensive Daily Prayer

Heavenly Father, I pray for myself, _____, _____, _____, and _____. I ask You to forgive us for all of our sins, iniquities, trespasses, transgressions, sins of commission, sins of omission and any other sins (listed on page 33 that apply to you) of: deception, desires of this world, disbelief, disdain, disobedience, dissension, division, divination, doubt, egoism, envy, false burdens, fantasy lust, fears, fornication, fretting, giving offense, gossip, greed, guilt, hard-hearted, heaviness, hate, haughtiness, hypocrisy, idolatry, impatience, indifferences, intimidation, intolerance, irritation, jealousy, judgmental, laboring, lasciviousness, legalism, lust, lust of the eye, lust of the flesh, lust of the mind, lying, manipulation, mis-belief, murder, plotting, presumption, pride, provoking, railing, rebellion, resentment, restlessness, rigidity, rudeness, sexual idolatry, sexual immorality, sexual impurity, sexual perversion, selfishness, self-centeredness, self-righteousness, self-criticalness, self-analysis, self-pity, strife, shame, slander, stiff necked, struggling, taking offense, tension, unbelief, uncleanness, undermining, unforgiveness, un-submissiveness, vanity, worry, worldly, wickedness, witchcraft, mischief, perfectionism, frustrations, addictions, dependencies, murmuring, complaining, petulance, all unrighteousness, etc, etc, etc; and any unknown sins according to Psalms 19:12. Heavenly Father, I repent for all of my sins and I ask You to forgive each of us for all our sins, iniquities, trespasses and transgressions and to cover them with the Blood of the Lord Christ Jesus, and to cleanse us of all unrighteousness. I ask You to do this in the Name of the Lord Christ Jesus of Nazareth according to Your Word, 1 John 1:9 and John 14:14.

Heavenly Father, I pray that You will give each of us all the things that I ask according to John 16:23 and I ask You Lord Jesus to do all things that I ask for each of us according to John 14:14.

I am thankful for this day; for this is the day that You have made. I will rejoice and be glad in it. I am thankful for the Blood of Jesus, knowing it cleanses us from all unrighteousness according to 1 John 1:9 and allows us to come boldly to the throne of grace according to Hebrews 4:16. I am thankful for the power in the Blood of the Lord Jesus Christ of Nazareth to protect, cleanse, heal, deliver, sanctify, redeem, justify, and to make all things new.

Heavenly Father, Your Word says that whatsoever I shall bind on earth shall be bound in heaven and whatsoever I loose on earth shall be loosed in heaven according to Matthew 16 and 18. In the Name of the Lord Jesus Christ I bind: all evil, wicked, demon, lying, unclean, tormenting, demonic spirits and strongmen in the Name of the Lord Jesus Christ of Nazareth. I bind them in my presence and everyone I just prayed for in the Name of the Lord Jesus Christ and I loose them to where Jesus sends them and I bind them and command them to stay there in the Name of Jesus Christ of Nazareth.

I apply the Blood of Jesus Christ of Nazareth over our homes according to Exodus 12:7. I apply the Blood of Jesus over every door and window of our homes. I apply the Blood of Jesus over all the contents of our homes. I apply the Blood of Jesus over all who enter in and all who exit out of our homes. Thank You Lord; for our homes and the Blood of Jesus over them.

I apply the Blood of Jesus over us as witnesses for You wherever we go. A city on a hill that cannot be hid. We will not hide our light under a bushel, but we will let our light shine before men and they may see our good works and glorify You Heavenly Father. We will give light to all those in our homes and our surroundings according to Matthew 5:14-16. Thank You Lord; for our ministries and the Blood of Jesus over them.

I apply the Blood of Jesus over our businesses and jobs. I apply the Blood of Jesus over our finances and possessions. I apply the Blood of Jesus over our bills, our checking accounts, and savings. I apply the Blood of Jesus over all of our possessions (list them) and everything we have and everything we will have. Thank You Lord; for our finances and possessions and the Blood of Jesus over them. I declare and decree that where the Blood of Jesus Christ is applied, satan can't enter according to Hebrews 10:4-23 and I confess now that Jesus is Lord over our families, churches, finances, businesses, jobs, and possessions. Not sickness, not poverty, not death, not problems, but Jesus is Lord over our families and our lives and where the power and presence of Jesus is: sickness, poverty, problems, and death can't remain.

Heavenly Father, I am thankful for so many things. I am thankful that Your Word is true and established in heaven according to Matthew 24:35; that Your mercy endures forever according to Psalms 118:1; that Your grace is sufficient for us according to 2 Corinthians 12:9; for Your angels and for Your protection according to Psalms 91; for Your salvation. That our names are written in the lamb's book of life according to Revelation 21:27; that everyone in our households are saved according to Acts 16:31; for Your righteousness that is imparted to us according to 1 Corinthians 5:21. I am thankful for Your Holy Spirit, the inward voice, the inward witness, the candle of the Lord according to Proverbs 20:27; that You sanctify us daily in Your Word according to John 17:17. Thank You for Your peace which passes all understanding according to Philippians 4:7. Thank You for every battle and every problem we face, knowing that the battle is an opportunity to cause our revelation knowledge parts (pebbles) to become one solid rock that the gates of hell can't prevail against us. Each and every battle is an opportunity for us to take root so we can bear fruit. We know that the trying of our faith turns into patience, causing us to form into perfect men and women, wanting nothing. Thank You that we can ask You for whatever we will and as long as we are connected to the vine, we have the petitions we ask for. Thank You for Your provisions as You supply all our needs according to Your riches in glory. Thank You for divine prosperity. Thank You for Your healing, past, present, and future as You are Jehovah Rophe. Thank You for divine health. Thank You for physical and spiritual hearing, seeing, feeling, smelling, and tasting. Thank You for the sun, moon, stars, trees, grass, air, water, plants, flowers, animals, mountains, valleys and all the other wonderful things You created for us yet we so often take for granted.

Thank You Heavenly Father for Your Holy Spirit. Thank You for being present with us always. Thank You for the gifts of the Spirit: The word of wisdom, word of knowledge, faith, gifts of healing, workings of miracles, prophesy, discerning of spirits, divers kinds of tongues and the interpretation of tongues according to 1 Corinthians 12:8-10. Thank You for the fruits of the Spirit: Love, joy, peace, long suffering, kindness, goodness, faithfulness, gentleness, and self control according to Galatians 5:22. Thank You for Your faithfulness. Thank You for being the Wonderful Counselor, Mighty God, Everlasting Father, Prince of Peace according to Isaiah 9:6; The Way, The Truth, The Life according to John 14:6; The Light according to John 8:12; The Door according to John 10:9; The Bread of Life according to John 6:35; The Good Shepherd according to John 10:11; The Redeemer according to Psalms 78:35; The King of Kings and the Lord of Lords according to Rev. 19:16. Heavenly Father, I praise and thank You for everything You have done, for everything You are doing, and for everything You are going to do. I bless You Lord.

Heavenly Father, I know that our battle is not with flesh and blood, but against principalities, against powers, against the rulers of darkness of this age, against spiritual wickedness in high places, therefore, I put on each of us the whole armor of God, that we may be able to withstand in the evil day, and having done all to stand. We will be strong in You, Lord, and in the power of Your might according to Ephesians 6:10-13. We have Christ in us, the hope of glory, according to Colossians 1:27, so we shall prevail because the battles are not ours, but Yours Lord according to 1 Samuel 17:47.

Heavenly Father, I now put on each of us the Breastplate of Righteousness according to Ephesians 6:14; and pray Your Word that we have hidden in our hearts, that we might not sin against You; because You made Christ who knew no sin to be sin for us, that we might become the righteousness of You, God, in Him. I acknowledge You God as our Jehovah Tsidkenu Your Word says it means our righteousness; (1st Corinthians 1:30) and Jehovah Mekaddishkem, our sanctifier.

Heavenly Father, I realize that our own self-righteousness is as filthy rags in Your eyes according to Isaiah 64:6; but Your Word says if we confess our sins, You are faithful and just to forgive our sins and to cleanse us from all unrighteousness according to I John 1:9. Heavenly Father, please forgive us for our sins. We want to be Your loving and obedient child. We want to be Your spotless bride, presented unto You in glorious splendor, without spot or wrinkle or any such thing according to Ephesians 5:27. We want to be holy and without blemish, through the washing of the water of Your Word according to Ephesians 5:26; and acknowledge You are our Jehovah Mekaddishkem, our sanctifier, and we want to be Your humble servant, to walk in love, forgiveness, and gentleness toward each other, showing the love of Christ as Your body according to Ephesians 5:2. Remind us that if we do this we will exit out from Your righteousness and enter back into our old self-righteous filthy rags. Help us to be a doer of Your Word, not just a hearer only, deceiving ourselves according to James 1:22, so we may act upon the revelation knowledge You gave us.

I crucify our flesh now according to Romans 8:13, as we die daily from self desires and live to do Your desires according to 1 Corinthians 15:31. In the Name of Christ Jesus, I command the mind of our flesh to shut up: Don't talk to us about sin for we are dead to sin according to Romans 6:2; Don't talk to us about condemnation, for there is no condemnation to us because we are in Christ according Romans 8:1; We walk after the Spirit and not after the flesh according to Romans 8:4; We have been healed by the stripes of Jesus according to Isaiah 53:5. We have been redeemed from the curse of the law according to Galatians 3:13; We are blessed when we come in and blessed when we go out. We are blessed in the city and blessed in the country. Our fruits, seed, land and storehouse are blessed. Everything we touch is blessed and it prospers according to Deuteronomy 28:3-6. All these blessings shall come upon us and overtake us, because we obey the Voice of the Lord our God. Thank You God that you did not give us the spirit of fear, but of power, and of love, and of a sound mind according to 2 Timothy 1:7.

Heavenly Father, Your Word says we are not to be deceived, that the unrighteous will not inherit the Kingdom of God, neither fornicators, nor idolaters, nor adulterers, nor homosexuals, nor sodomites, nor thieves, nor covetous, nor drunkards, nor revilers, nor extortioners, according to 1 Corinthians 6:9-10. Your word continues to say; and such were some of us. But we were washed, but we were sanctified, but we were justified in the Name of the Lord Jesus and by the Spirit of God according to 1 Corinthians 6:11.

Heavenly Father, I pray that our path is like the shining sun and not of darkness for Your Word says: But the path of the just is like the shining sun, that shines ever brighter unto the perfect day. The way of the wicked is like darkness; they do not know why they stumble according to Proverbs 4:18-19. Your Word is a lamp unto our feet and a light unto our path according to Psalms 119:105.

Lord, You have created a clean heart in us; You have renewed a right spirit within us. You have made old things passed away and all things new. You didn't cast us away from Your presence and You didn't take Your Holy Spirit away from us when we failed You for Your mercy endures forever. You restored us to the joy of Your salvation according to Psalms 51:10-13. Your joy is our strength according to Nehemiah 8:10.

Heavenly Father, I now put on each of us the Helmet of Salvation. I declare that we are spiritually minded according to Romans 8:6 and have the mind of Christ according to 1 Corinthians 2:16. I take off the carnal way of thinking according to Romans 12:2. Putting on this Helmet we no longer allow our five carnal senses to affect the way that we think. I exercise our spiritual senses, spiritual hearing, spiritual sight, spiritual touch, spiritual taste, and spiritual smell according to Romans 8:14. I thank You for being our God of peace; Jehovah Shalom, according to Judges 6:24.

Heavenly Father, I ask that You give us knowledge of Your will in all wisdom and spiritual understanding and the strength and might of You, to be involved in what you want us to be involved in, and not to be involved in the things You don't want us to be involved in according to Colossians 1:9. Your Word says if any man lacks wisdom, let him ask of You, and he will receive wisdom according to James 1:5. I ask for wisdom in every decision we have to make today. Help us to remember that our mind is a judge according to 1 Corinthians 11:31 and we are always listening to fear or faith. Fear produces substances of things not hoped for, the evidence of this world's circumstances: evidence of things we can hear, see, smell, taste, and touch. These things are temporal according to 2 Corinthians 4:18. God did not give us a spirit of fear according to 2 Timothy 1:7. Faith produces substances of things hoped for, the evidence of things from the Word of God ("Thus saith the Lord.."): things we cannot hear, see, smell, touch or taste according to Hebrews 11:1. Now these things are eternal. From both of these reports, we choose to believe the report of the Lord according to 2 Timothy 1:12.

Heavenly Father, I ask that each of us will hear Your Voice today for our families according to John 10:16: That we will not be deceived in any area, that You will speak through us to our families, and that we will follow You and set a clear path for our families to follow according to John 16:13-15. Let the words of our mouths and the meditation of our hearts be acceptable in Your sight, for You are our strength and our redeemer according to Psalms 19:14. Let our mouths speak wisdom and the meditation of our hearts be of understanding according to Psalms 19:3. Let our speech always be with grace, seasoned with salt, that we will know how to answer every man according to Colossians 4:6. Give us the tongue of the learned and lead us to speak a word to him that is weary in season according to Isaiah 50:4. Teach us to exhort one another today, lest anyone of us be hardened through the deceitfulness of sin according to Hebrews 3:13. Help us to never criticize, condemn, or complain because these are destructive weapons that kill, steal, and destroy. They are weapons of the enemy according to John 10:10. Help us to abstain from all appearances of evil according to 1 Thessalonians 5:19-22.

Heavenly Father, implant in our hearts: We are doers of the Word according to James 1:22; We are in Jesus and Jesus is in us according to John 17:23; We are the body of Christ according to 1 Corinthians 12:27; We are more than conquerors through Christ Jesus according to Romans 8:37. We are overcomers. We overcome by the Blood of Jesus and the word of our testimony and we love not our life unto death according to Revelation 12:11; We are the head and not the tail according to Deuteronomy 28:13; We can do all things through Christ who strengthens us according to Philippians 4:13; As we speak Your Word, we know it won't return back to You void, but it will accomplish what it was sent to do according to Isaiah 55:11; If we ask anything according to Your will, You hear us, and because You hear us, we have whatsoever it is we ask for according to 1 John 5:14-15.

Heavenly Father, I thank You for it is written in Psalms 103 that we will not forget all of Your benefits. You forgave all our sins and have healed all our diseases, You redeemed our lives from destruction. You have crowned us with loving kindness and tender mercies; You satisfy our mouths with good things, so that our youth is renewed like the eagles; You are merciful and gracious, slow to anger, and plenteous in mercy; You have not dealt with us according to our iniquities; As far as the heaven is high above the earth, so great is Your mercy toward us for we fear You; As far as the east is from the west, You have thrown our sins from us.

Heavenly Father, I now gird our loins with Your Belt of Truth. We are set free from bondages and strongholds according to II Corinthians 10:4. We operate in discernment according to Hebrews 5:14 that we may continue to be free. I take off all dependency of the flesh and dependency on anything in this world or this world system. We trust and depend completely on Jesus according to Psalms 31:1. I thank You that You are our Healer, Jehovah Rophe, and You are our Provider; Jehovah Jireh.

Heavenly Father, thank You for being our Healer, our Jehovah Rophe according to Exodus 15:26. I declare that You are our health, healing, and soundness in and over us. We have the healing of God, for by Your stripes, we were healed according to I Peter 2:24. We have spiritual healing, soulish healing, physical healing, healing in relationships for we have been redeemed from the curse of the law according to Galatians 3:13. We have been redeemed from sickness, poverty, and spiritual death according to Deuteronomy 28:2-13. We have the health of God. We have Your soundness in our spirits, souls, and bodies. We present our bodies as living sacrifices, holy and acceptable to You, which is our reasonable service. We are not conformed to this world, but we are transformed by the renewing of our minds to Your Word according to Romans 12:1-2. Lord, You are on our side. We fear no man according to Psalms 118:6. We are overcomers. We overcome all strongholds and bondages by the Blood of the Lamb, which cleanses us from all unrighteousness according to 1 John 1:9 and the word of our testimony which is Your Word that we have hidden in our hearts to keep us from returning to those strongholds according to Psalms 119:11 and we love not our life unto death according to Revelation 12:11.

Heavenly Father, thank You that all of Your blessings will come on us because we hear and obey Your Voice. Thank You that: Blessed is the fruit of our bodies (our children); Blessed is the fruit of our ground (our possessions); Blessed is the fruit of our cattle (our businesses); Blessed is the increase of our kine (our prosperity); Blessed are the flocks of our sheep (those we have authority over); Blessed is our basket and our store (our finances). Lord, You have commanded blessings on us, our storehouse and in all we set our hands to. You have blessed us in the land that You gave us. You have established us as a holy people unto You as You promised us, as we keep Your commandments and walk in Your ways. We are blessed because we refuse to walk in the counsel of the ungodly, nor will we stand in the way of sinners, nor will we sit in the seat of the scornful. Our delight is in Your Word, and on Your Word do we meditate day and night. We are like a tree planted by rivers of water that bring forth its fruit in its season; our leaves shall not wither, and whatsoever we do shall prosper according to Psalms 1:1-3. We bring all our tithes into Your storehouse, that there may be meat in Your house, and I will prove You now that You will open the windows of heaven for us and pour out blessings that we won't have room to store it all so we will have to give most of it away. For as we have received; freely we shall give according to Matthew 10:8.

Lord, Your goodness and mercy shall follow us every day of our lives according to Psalms 23:6. In You, we will praise Your Word and put our trust according to Psalms 16:1. We will not fear what flesh and blood can do to us according to Ephesians 6:12. We know that all things work together for good because we love You and we were called according to Your purpose according to Romans 8:28. According to Romans 8:31, if You are for us; who can be against us? You are on our side; we will not fear what man can do to us, according to Psalms 118:6. Now Lord, bring our requests to You according to Philippians 4:6: (Prayer List)

Heavenly Father, I now cover our feet with the preparation of the Gospel of Peace Sandals, enabling us to walk in the Spirit so we won't fulfill the lust of the flesh according to Galatians 5:16. Thank You that the Spirit leads us and we walk in the light, as Jesus is, the light according to 1 John 1:7. As we cover our feet with this preparation, we take off vanity, pride, darkness, and ignorance according to Colossians 3:8-10. I thank You for being: our EVER PRESENT GOD, our JEHOVAH SHAMMAH and our SHEPHERD, JEHOVAH ROHI.

Lord, Your Spirit is upon us. You have anointed us to preach the gospel to the poor; You have sent us to bind up the broken hearted, to proclaim liberty to the captives, and the opening of the prison to them that are bound; To proclaim Your acceptable year, and Your day of vengeance; To comfort all that mourn; To appoint unto them that mourn in Zion, to give unto them beauty for ashes, the oil of joy for mourning, the garment of praise for the spirit of heaviness; that they might be called trees of righteousness, which is Your planting, that You may be glorified.

Heavenly Father, I ask that utterance be given to us, that we may open our mouths boldly to make known the mysteries of the Gospel, for which we are ambassadors in chains, that in it we may speak boldly, as we ought to speak according to Ephesians 6:19-20.

Heavenly Father, I ask that You order our steps according to Psalms 37:23. We acknowledge You Father, precious Jesus, and precious Holy Spirit in all our ways, according to Proverbs 3:6. I acknowledge You Jesus as Lord over all our ways and in everything we do, we will do it heartily according to Colossians 3:23, listening to Your Spirit and rejoicing as we do it for You. We have Your promise that You will direct our path according to Proverbs 4:18. We will not lean to our own understanding, go by what we think is good, but we will trust Your Holy Spirit with all our heart and will believe our path is directed by You according to Proverbs 3:5-6.

Heavenly Father, I speak in Jesus' Name to every person and thing in our paths, that if it would not bring glory to You God, and if it would not be in Your will for our paths to cross, then in Jesus' Name, I forbid our paths to cross until, if ever, it would be in God's will. Also, I speak in Jesus' Name and believe for every person and things in our path that would be in God's will and for God's glory for our paths to cross, I speak and believe for our paths to cross in God's right timing. I declare KINGDOM OF GOD COME, WILL OF GOD BE DONE IN EVERY STEP WE TAKE AND WITH EVERY PERSON WE MEET. Truly all things work together for good for us because we love You Lord, and we are called according to Your purpose according to Romans 8:28.

Heavenly Father, we do not seek after the praises of men according to John 5:44, nor do we seek after our own glory according to John 7:18, but we seek first Your kingdom; we seek after Your righteousness according to Matthew 6:33. Your Spirit leads us, as You are Jehovah Rohi, our shepherd according to Psalms 23:1. Instruct us and teach us in the way we should go. Guide us with Your eye according to Psalms 32:8. Holy Spirit guide us into all truth, speak to us the words that you hear from our Heavenly Father and tell us the things to come. Glorify God in us by taking the things of God and declaring it to us according to John 16:13-14. We will keep Your word, Lord, make Your home in us. Teach us all things, and help us to remember all things You have taught us according to John 14:26.

Heavenly Father, we want to be wise sons and daughters who gather the harvest instead of sons and daughters who cause You shame and sleep during the harvest according to Proverbs 10:5. Help us to keep a right heart and a hearing ear according to Proverbs 20:12. Give us wisdom to use You to win Your people to Your kingdom. Lead us to them and tell us what to say that they may be saved according to Acts 1:8. We are not ashamed of Your Gospel for it is the power of You, God, unto salvation according to Romans 1:16. Give Your servants boldness to stand up for You and tell others what You have done for us according to Acts 4:29. Help us to make disciples for You, for where no counsel is, the people fall, but in a multitude of counselors, there is safety according to Proverbs 11:14. We want to be vehicles for Your Holy Spirit. Lead us into the north, south, east, and west. Help us to bring them and lead them out of darkness into Your light according to 1 Peter 2:9. I believe You are adding to Your church daily such as should be saved according to Acts 2:47. We go forth to do Your will. We go into the entire world that You have called us to and preach Your gospel according to Mark 16:15. We go rejoicing in hope, patient in tribulation, continuing instantly in prayer, and distributing to the necessity of the saints according to Romans 12:12-13. We will walk worthy of our calling with all lowliness and gentleness, with longsuffering, bearing with one another in love, enduring to keep the unity of Your Spirit in the bond of peace according to Ephesians 4:1-3. We will not follow after signs to believe on our Word, but rather signs will follow us because we believe on Your Word according to Mark 16:17.

Heavenly Father, I now put on each of us the Shield of Faith, which protects us from all fiery darts of the enemy according to Ephesians 6: As I put on each of us the Shield of Faith, we take off all fear, mistrust, unthankfulness, unfaithfulness, and disobedience. I thank You God that You are OUR BANNER, JEHOVAH NISSI and THE GOD WHO IS MORE THAN ENOUGH, EL SHADDAI.

Heavenly Father, I come boldly to the throne of grace according to Hebrews 4:16, praying for all men. I ask that every man, woman, boy, and girl will come to know You as their Lord and Savior according to 1 Timothy 2:1. Let everything that has breath praise You according to Psalms 150:6.

Heavenly Father, I pray that Your Kingdom come, Your will be done over our families. I ask You to make Your Word stronger and greater than our wills. I ask You to make us hunger and thirst after our righteousness according to Matthew 5:6. I stand on Your promises that (list children) will prophesy according to Acts 2:17. I intercede in the Spirit that our families are saved by faith. Help each of us to keep a pure heart according to 1 Peter 1:22. Keep us in remembrance of Your promise that You will never leave us or forsake us according to Hebrews 13:5. I take the Shield of Faith and cover our families, and churches: For You will bless the righteous with favor and protect us; surrounding us with a shield according to Psalms 5:12.

Heavenly Father, I declare that we dwell in Your secret place and we abide under Your shadow, I declare that You are our refuge and our fortress, You are our habitation, therefore no demon, devil, fallen angel, principalities, rulers of darkness, power, spiritual wickedness, satan, or those under him shall befall us, neither shall any plague, flu, virus, cancer, disease, headache, cold or poverty come near our dwellings. A thousand may fall at our side, and ten thousand at our right hand, but it will not, shall not, and cannot come near our dwellings because I now apply the Blood of Jesus to the doorpost of our hearts. You have given Your angels charge over us to keep us in all our ways, lest we dash our foot against a stone, with long life You satisfy us and show us Your salvation, because we have set our love upon You according to Psalms 91:1-16.

Heavenly Father, I ask that (church) becomes a great soul winning church for You. I pray for Pastor _____ and ask You to bless him/her. Bless (church) financially to have and maintain abundant provision, to fulfill Your mission for us. Help us to have Your abundance to give as we are led by Your Spirit in giving to others. Make our leaders sensitive to You and the needs of our children and our youth, making them grow mightily in the ways and things of God according to Ephesians 4:15, making them giants for You. Bring a great revival so we will be strong in You and in the power of Your might according to Ephesians 6:10. Let us recognize sin immediately and turn from it. Let us walk in love according to Ephesians 5:2 and desire spiritual things according to Colossians 3:2.

Heavenly Father, I now intercede for those You have called me to intercede for. I pray the will of God be done in and over me and everyone I have prayed for today. Strengthen us today and clothe us with Your glory. Let us hear Your Voice today and teach us in Your ways. Keep each of us covered in Your Blood and heal us of every sickness and disease that the devil tries to hit us with. I cover each of us with the Shield of Faith and declare that no weapon formed against us shall prosper, but everything we put our hands to shall prosper, for we are like a tree planted by rivers water according to Psalms 1:3.

Heavenly Father, I now put in each of our hands the Sword of the Spirit, the Word of God, which we choose to use against all forces of evil. I declare that we defeat the enemy with the Word of God as the Spirit of God leads us according to Revelation 19:11-16. I put away murmuring, complaining, condemning and criticizing from each of us. I thank You that You are OUR AUTHORITY, JESUS and THE LORD OF HOSTS, JEHOVAH SABBOATH. I now take the Sword of the Spirit and use the authority that God has ordained me with according to Luke 9:1, for we have been given power and authority over all the devils and demons, to tread upon serpents and scorpions, and over all the power of the enemy according to Luke 10:19.

Heavenly Father, as we go out today, let us recognize You as Jehovah Sabaoth, we will not fear, for You have called us by name, we are Yours. When we pass through the waters, You will be with us, and through the rivers, they will not overtake us. When we walk through the fire, we will not be burned, neither will the flame kindle upon us according to Isaiah 43:1-2. We will not be dismayed, for You are our God according to Isaiah 41:10. We will wait upon You Lord and You will renew our strength. We will mount up with wings as eagles. We will run and not be weary. We will walk and not faint according to Isaiah 40:31. We will not be afraid or dismayed by reason of the great multitude. The battle is not ours but Yours according to II Chronicles 20:15. You are on our side; therefore we will fear no man according to Psalms 118:6. When the enemy comes in like a flood, Your Spirit will lift up a standard against him according to Isaiah 59:19. You did not give us a spirit of fear, but of power, and of love, and of a sound mind according to 2 Timothy 1:7. Greater is Jesus in us than any demon, devil, fallen angel, evil force, power, principality, and rulers of darkness, spiritual wickedness, satan, and those under him. Greater is Jesus in us than the devil is in the world according to I John 4:4. Greater is Jesus in us than all our circum stances and all our reasoning. Therefore, we follow You Jesus. We cry out to You Holy, Holy, Holy, Lord God Almighty, who was, who is, and who is to come according to Revelation 4:8. You have created all things and for Your pleasure and by Your will, they are and were created and continue to exist. You are worthy to receive glory, honor, and power according to Revelation 4:11. To You belongs the kingdom, and the power, and the glory forever according to Matthew 6:13. Amen.

Disabling Strongmen Prayer

Prayer of Loosing Strongmen

Heavenly Father, I (we) come to You now in the Name of my (our) Lord and Savior Christ Jesus. Holy Spirit I (we) pray that You will quicken me (us) to hear my (our) Heavenly Father's Voice and to lead me (us) in prayer. Heavenly Father, I (we) bow and worship before You. I (we) come to You with praise and with thanksgiving. I (we) come to You in humility, in fear, in trembling and seeking truth. I (we) come to You in gratitude, in love, and through the precious Blood of Your Son Jesus Christ of Nazareth.

Strongman called spirit of rejection, spirit of anti-christ, spirit of error, spirit of seducing spirit, spirit of bondage, spirit of death, spirit of divination, spirit of dumb and deaf, spirit of familiar spirit, spirit of fear, spirit of pride, spirit of Leviathan, spirit of heaviness, spirit of infirmity, spirit of jealousy, spirit of lying, spirit of perverse spirit, and spirit of whoredoms; I rebuke you and bind you in the Name of the Lord Jesus Christ, along with all of your works, roots, fruits, tentacles, links, that are in my (our) presence, the presence of anybody I (we) have prayed for today, every organ, every cell, every gland, every muscle, every ligament, every bone in our bodies, our houses, cars, trucks, buildings, properties, and pets, and I loose you to go where Jesus Christ sends you. I apply the Blood of Jesus Christ over myself, each person I (we) prayed for today, our houses, cars, properties, offices, work places, and pets as our protection.

Lord Jesus Christ, we ask You to destroy any familiar spirit that has allowed any of these demonic strongmen into our presence. In the Name of the Lord Jesus Christ according to John 14:14.

I declare in the Name of Jesus Christ that all of your works, roots, fruits, tentacles, and links are now dead works in our lives. I declare that your power over us is broken. Heavenly Father, I ask you in the Name of Jesus to break all generational and word curses that we have placed on ourselves or by others in the Name of Jesus.

Heavenly Father, I ask You to loose into each of us: the Spirit of Adoption (Romans 8:15), the Spirit of Truth (l John 4:6, Psalms 51:10), the Holy Spirit of Truth (John 16:13), the Spirit of Resurrection Life and Life more Abundantly (John 11:25, John 10:10b), the Holy Spirit and His Gifts (1 Corinthians 12:9-12).

Heavenly Father, I (we) ask You to fill each of us with Your precious Holy Spirit. I (we) ask You to fill each of us with all of the fruits of Your Holy Spirit including Your love, Your joy, Your peace, Your gentleness, Your goodness, Your meekness, Your faithfulness and Your self-control. Heavenly Father, in Christ Jesus' Holy Name I (we) ask You to fill me (us), everyone I (we) prayed for today with Your Holy Ghost anointing and power, cover us with Your presence, Your anointing, Your power; in the Name of Jesus Christ of Nazareth.

Heavenly Father, I (we) bow and worship and praise before You and I (we) apply the Blood of Jesus Christ over myself (ourselves), each person that I (we) have prayed for today; from the tops of our heads to the soles of our feet. I (we) apply the Blood of Jesus over the airways that surround us, over telephone lines, over our homes, properties, offices, cars, trucks, businesses, finances, marriages, ministries, cell phone frequencies . . . I (we) apply the precious Blood of Christ Jesus as our protection and I (we) ask You to render powerless and harmless and nullify the power, destroy the power, cancel the power of any evil spirit, demonic spirit, demonic strongman, messenger of satan that tries to come into our presence, everything in our homes, our pets, our properties, everything in our cars and trucks, our marriages, our finances, our ministries, our telephone lines, our cell phone frequencies . . . in the Name of Jesus Christ of Nazareth. Amen!

Spirit of Rejection

Genesis 3:6-13

"Strongman called Spirit of Rejection, I bind you in the Name of Jesus Christ along with all of your works, roots, fruits, tentacles, links and spirits that are in my life __________, __________, __________, __________, and the lives of everybody I have prayed for today, along with all of your fruits and spirits of:

Rejection by Others	Self-Rejection
Rejection of Others	Rejection of God

And I cast you out of me, __________, __________, __________, and everybody I have prayed for today along with all of your works, roots, fruits, tentacles, links and spirits, and I loose you from us and I force you into outer darkness in the Name of Jesus Christ.

I bind you in the Name of Jesus Christ and declare that all of your works, roots, fruits, tentacles, links, and spirits, are dead works in my life __________, __________, __________, __________, and the lives of everybody I have prayed for today, in Jesus Christ' Name, and I bind you and loose you from me, everybody I prayed for today and I loose you to go wherever Jesus Christ sends you and command you not to come back into our presence again. I ask You, Heavenly Father, to loose into me and each person I prayed for today the Spirit of Adoption according to Romans 8:15. Amen

Bind: Spirit of Rejection
Loose: Spirit of Adoption
Romans 8:15

Spirit of Anti-Christ

1 John 4:3

"Strongman called Spirit of Anti-Christ, I bind you in the Name of Jesus Christ along with all of your works, roots, fruits, tentacles, links and spirits that are in my life, __________, __________, __________, __________, and the lives of everybody I have prayed for today, along with all of your fruits and spirits of:

Denies the Deity of Christ
I John 4:3
2 John 7

Denies the Atoning Blood of
Jesus
1 John 4:3

Against Christ & His
Teachings
2 Thessalonians 2:4
1 John 4:3

Humanism
2 Thessalonians 2:3.7

Worldly Speech & Actions
1 John 4:5

Teachers of Heresies
1 John 2:18,19

Anti-Christian
Revelation 13.7

Deceiver
2 Thessalonians 2:4
2 John 7

Lawlessness/Rebellion
2 Thessalonians 2:3-12

And I cast you out of me, __________, __________, __________, and everybody I have prayed for today along with all of your works, roots, fruits, tentacles, links and spirits, and I loose you from us and I force you into outer darkness in the Name of Jesus Christ.

I bind you in the Name of Jesus Christ and declare that all of your works, roots, fruits, tentacles, links, and spirits, are dead works in my life __________, __________, __________, __________, and the lives of everybody I have prayed for today. in Jesus Christ' Name, and I bind you and I loose you to go wherever Jesus Christ sends you and command you not to come back into our presence again. I ask You, Heavenly Father, to loose into me and each person I prayed for today the Spirit of Truth according to I John 4:6. Amen
Bind: Spirit of Anti-Christ
Loose: Spirit of Truth
1 John 4:6

Spirit of Error

I John 4:6

"Strongman called Spirit of Error, I bind you in the Name of Jesus Christ along with all of your works, roots, fruits, tentacles, links and spirits that are in my life __________, __________, __________, __________, and the lives of everybody I have prayed for today, along with all of your fruits and spirits of:

Resistance to Biblical
Truths & Spiritual
Hindrances to Prayer,
Bible Study,
Listening to Sermons
& Moving in the Gifts of The Holy Spirit

Error
Proverbs 14:33
1 John 4:6
2 Peter 3:16,17

Reprobate Mind, Deceit
Foolish Talking

Unsubmissive
Proverbs 29:1
1 John 4:6

Mental Confusion, Fears
Physical Illnesses &
Pains Depression,
Dullness of
Comprehension

False Doctrines
1 Timothy 6:20,21
2 Timothy 4:3

Titus 3:10
1 John 4:1-6

Unteachable
Proverbs 10:17; 12:1;
13:18;15:10,12,32
2 Timothy 4:1-4
1 John 4:6

Profanity

Servant of Corruption
2 Peter 2:19

Defensive/Argumentative

Having a Form of
Godliness
Variance

Contentions
James 3:16

Uncleanness

New Age Movement
2 Thessalonians
2 Peter 2:10

And I cast you out of me __________, __________, __________, and everyone I have prayed for today along with all of your works, roots, fruits, tentacles, links and spirits, and I loose you from us and I force you into outer darkness in the Name of Jesus Christ.

I bind you in the Name of Jesus Christ and declare that all of your works, roots, fruits, tentacles, links, and spirits, are dead works in my life ______ ______, __________, __________, __________, and everyone I have prayed for today in Jesus Christ' Name, and I bind you and loose you from me, everyone I have prayed for today and I loose you to go wherever Jesus Christ sends you and command you not to come back into our presence again. I ask You, Heavenly Father, to loose into me and into each person I have prayed for today the Spirit of Truth according to I John 4:6 and Psalm 51:10. Amen

Bind: Spirit of Error
Loose: Spirit of Truth
1 John 4:6; Psalm 51:10

Seducing Spirits

1 Timothy 4:1

"Strongman called Seducing Spirits, I bind you in the Name of Jesus Christ along with all of your works, roots, fruits, tentacles, links and spirits that are in my life __________, __________, __________, __________, and the lives of everybody I have prayed for today, along with all of your fruits and spirits of:

Hypocritical Lies
I Timothy 4:11
Proverbs 12:22

Seared Conscience
1Timothy 4:1
James 1:14

Attractions / Fascination to
False Prophets, Signs &
Wonders
Mark 13:22

Deception
Romans 7:11
2 Timothy 3:13
2 Thessalonians 2:10
1 John 2:18-26

Confusion

Wander From The Truth
2 Timothy 3:13

Fascination to Evil Ways, Objects or Persons
Proverbs 12:26

Seducers—Enticers
1 Timothy 4:1
2 Timothy 3:13
Proverbs 1:10

Controlling spirit (Jezebel)

And I cast you out of me __________, __________, __________, and everybody I have prayed for today along with all of your works, roots, fruits, tentacles, links and spirits, and I loose you from us and I force you into outer darkness in the Name of Jesus Christ.

I bind you in the Name of Jesus Christ and declare that all of your works, roots, fruits, tentacles, links, and spirits, are dead works in my life __________, __________, __________, __________, and the lives of everybody I have prayed for today, in Jesus Christ' Name, and I bind you and loose you from me, everybody I have prayed for today and I loose you to go wherever Jesus Christ sends you and command you not to come back into our presence again. I ask You, Heavenly Father, to loose into me and each person I prayed for today the Holy Spirit of Truth according to John 16:13. Amen
Bind: Seducing Spirits
Loose: Holy Spirit of Truth
John 16:13

Spirit of Bondage

Romans 8:15

"Strongman called Spirit of Bondage, I bind you in the Name of Jesus Christ along with all of your works, roots, fruits, tentacles, links and spirits that are in my life __________, __________, __________, __________, and the lives of everybody I have prayed for today, along with all of your fruits and spirits of:

Fears
Romans 8:15

Addictions to Drugs,
Alcohol, Cigarettes, Sleep,
Sex Food, Pornography, etc.

Fear of Death/Dying
Hebrews 2:14,15

Captivity to Satan
2 Peter 2:19

Compulsive Sin
Proverbs 5:22
John 8:34
Servant of Corruption
Luke 8:26-29
John 8:34
Acts 8:23

Bondage to Sin
2 Timothy 2:26

And I cast you out of me __________, __________, __________, and everybody I have prayed for today along with all of your works, roots, fruits, tentacles, links and spirits, and I loose you from us and I force you into outer darkness in the Name of Jesus Christ.

I bind you in the Name of Jesus Christ and declare that all of your works, roots, fruits, tentacles, links, and spirits, are dead works in my life __________, __________, __________, __________, and the lives of everybody I have prayed for today, in Jesus Christ' Name, and I bind you and loose you from me, everybody I have prayed for today and I loose you to go wherever Jesus Christ sends you and command you not to come back into our presence again. I ask You, Heavenly Father, to loose into me and each person I have prayed for today Liberty and the Spirit of Adoption according to Romans 8:15. Amen

Bind: Spirit of Bondage

Loose: Liberty, Spirit of Adoption

Romans 8:15

Spirit of Death
1 Corinthians 15:26

"Strongman called Spirit of Death, I bind you in the Name of Jesus Christ along with all of your works, roots, fruits, tentacles, links and spirits that are in my life, ________, ________, ________, ________, and lives of everybody I have prayed for today, along with all of your fruits and spirits of:

Murder
Genesis 4:8

Suicide

Accidents

Fear of Death/Dying

Anger That Leads to Death

Near Death Experiences

Miscarriages

Abortion
Exodus 20:13; 21:2-25

Barrenness

And I cast you out of me ________, ________, ________, and everybody I have prayed for today along with all of your works, roots, fruits, tentacles, links and spirits, and I loose you from us and I force you into outer darkness in the Name of Jesus Christ.

I bind you in the Name of Jesus Christ and declare that all of your works, roots, fruits, tentacles, links, and spirits, are dead works in my life ___________, ___________, ___________, ___________, and the lives of everybody I have prayed for today, in Jesus Christ' Name, and I bind you and loose you from me, everybody I have prayed for today and I loose you to go wherever Jesus Christ sends you and command you not to come back into our presence again. I ask You, Heavenly Father, to loose into me and each person I have prayed for today the Resurrection Life and Life More Abundantly according to John 11:25; John 10:10b. Amen

Bind: Spirit of Death
Loose: Resurrection Life and Life More Abundantly
John 11:25; John 10:10b

Spirit of Divination

Acts 16:16-18

"Strongman called Spirit of Divination, I bind you in the Name of Jesus Christ along with all of your works, roots, fruits, tentacles, links and spirits that are in my life __________, __________, __________, __________, and the lives of everybody I have prayed for today, along with all of your fruits and spirits of:

Fortuneteller-Soothsayer
Micah 5:12
Isaiah 2:6
Stargazer-zodiac,
Horoscopes, Astrology
Isaiah 47:13
Leviticus 19:26
Jeremiah 10:2
Warlock-Witch, Sorcerer
Exodus 22:18
Hypnotist-Enchanter
Deuteronomy 18:11
Isaiah 19:3
Rebellion
1 Samuel 15:23

Manipulation & Control
Water Witching—Divination
Hosea 4:12
Drugs (Pharmakos)
Galatians 5:20
Revelation 9:21; 18:23; 21:8;
22:15
Astral Projecting, Levitation,
Seances, Dungeons & Dragons
Magic
Exodus 7:11; 8:7; 9:11

Tarot Cards, Ouija Boards,
Palm Reading, Crystal Balls
Haughtiness, Pride, Arrogance,
Ego, Vanity

And I cast you out of me, __________, __________, __________, and everybody I have prayed for today along with all of your works, roots, fruits, tentacles, links and spirits, and I loose you from us and I force you into outer darkness in the Name of Jesus Christ.

I bind you in the Name of Jesus Christ and declare that all of your works, roots, fruits, tentacles, links, and spirits, are dead works in my life __________, __________, __________, __________, and the lives of everybody I have prayed for today, in Jesus Christ' Name, and I bind you and loose you from me, everybody I have prayed for today and I loose you to go wherever Jesus Christ sends you and command you not to come back into our presence again. I ask You, Heavenly Father, to loose into me and each person I have prayed for today the Holy Spirit and His Gifts according to 1 Corinthians 2:9-12. Amen
Bind: Spirit of Divination
Loose: Holy Spirit and His Gifts
1 Corinthians 12:9-12

Dumb and Deaf Spirit

Mark 9:17-29

"Strongman called Dumb & Deaf Spirit, I bind you in the Name of Jesus Christ along with all of your works, roots, fruits, tentacles, links and spirits that are in my life __________, __________, __________, __________, and the lives of everybody I have prayed for today, along with all of your fruits and spirits of:

Dumb-Mute
Mark 9:25
Matthew 9:32,33; 12:22;
15:30,31
Luke 11:14
Isaiah 35:5,6
Crying
Mark 9:26
Drown
Mark 9:22
Tearing
Mark 9:18,20,26
Mental Illness
Matthew 17:15
Mark 5:5; 9:17
Blindness
Matthew 12:22

Suicidal
Mark 9:22
Foaming at The Mouth
Mark 9:39
Luke 9:39
Ear Problems
Mark 9:25,26
Seizures/Epilepsy
Mark 9:18,20,26

Burn
Mark 9:22
Gnashing of Teeth
Mark 9:39
Pining Away, Prostration
Mark 9:18,26
Madness/Insanity, Senility
Schizophrenia, Paranoia
Self-Mutilation

And I cast you out of me ____________, ____________, ____________, ____________, and everybody I have prayed for today along with all of your works, roots, fruits, tentacles, links and spirits, and I loose you from us and I force you into outer darkness in the Name of Jesus Christ.

I bind you in the Name of Jesus Christ and declare that all of your works, roots, fruits, tentacles, links, and spirits, are dead works in my life ____________, ____________, ____________, ____________, and the lives of everybody I have prayed for today, in Jesus Christ' Name, and I bind you and loose you from me, everybody I have prayed for today and I loose you to go wherever Jesus Christ sends you and command you not to come back into our presence again. I ask You, Heavenly Father, to loose into me and each person I have prayed for today the Resurrection Life and Gifts of Healing according to Romans 8:11 and 1 Corinthians 12:9-12. Amen
Bind: Dumb and Deaf Spirit
Loose: Resurrection Life and Gifts of Healing
Romans 8:11; 1 Corinthians 12:9-12

Familiar Spirit

Leviticus 19:31

"Strongman called Familiar Spirit, I bind you in the Name of Jesus Christ along with all of your works, roots, fruits, tentacles, links and spirits that are in my life ________, ________, ________, ________, and the lives of everybody I have prayed for today, along with all of your fruits and spirits of:

Necromancer
Deuteronomy 18:11
1 Chronicles 10:13

ESP, Mind Readers, TM
Psychics

Medium
1 Samuel 28

Yoga
Jeremiah 29:8

Peeping & Muttering
Isaiah 8:19; 29:4; 59:3

Spiritist
1 Samuel 28

Clairvoyant
1 Samuel 28:7,8

Apathy
Passive Mind-Dreamers
Jeremiah 23:16,25,32; 27:9,10

Drugs (Pharmakos)
Revelation 9:21; 18:23; 21:8;
22:15

False Prophecies
Isaiah 8:19, 29:4

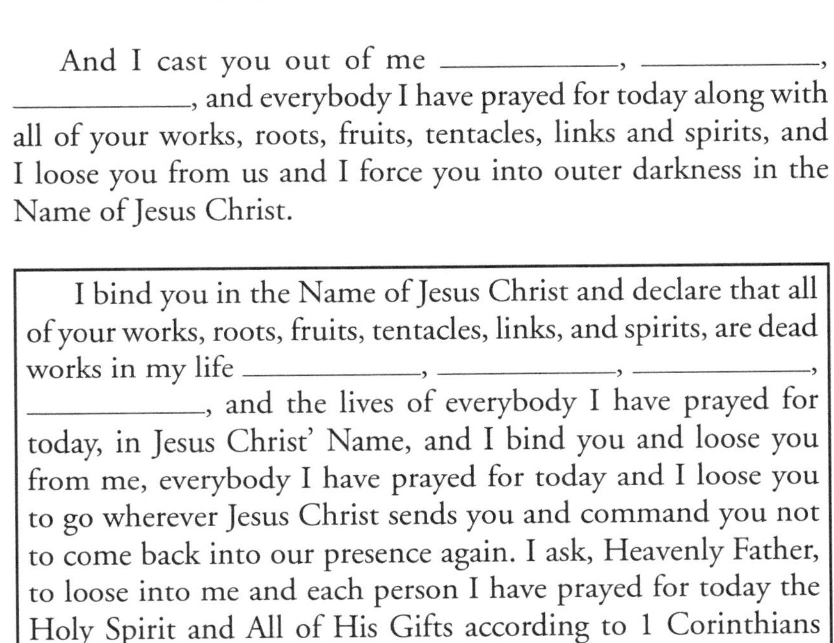

And I cast you out of me __________, __________, __________, and everybody I have prayed for today along with all of your works, roots, fruits, tentacles, links and spirits, and I loose you from us and I force you into outer darkness in the Name of Jesus Christ.

I bind you in the Name of Jesus Christ and declare that all of your works, roots, fruits, tentacles, links, and spirits, are dead works in my life __________, __________, __________, __________, and the lives of everybody I have prayed for today, in Jesus Christ' Name, and I bind you and loose you from me, everybody I have prayed for today and I loose you to go wherever Jesus Christ sends you and command you not to come back into our presence again. I ask, Heavenly Father, to loose into me and each person I have prayed for today the Holy Spirit and All of His Gifts according to 1 Corinthians 12:9-12. Amen

Bind: Familiar Spirit
Loose: Holy Spirit and All Of His Gifts
1 Corinthians 12:9-12

Spirit of Fear

2 Timothy 1:7

"Strongman called Spirit of Fear, I bind you in the Name of Jesus Christ along with all of your works, roots, fruits, tentacles, links and spirits that are in my life __________, __________, __________, __________, and the lives of everybody I have prayed for today, along with all of your fruits and spirits of:

Fears –
Phobias
Isaiah 13:7,8
2 Timothy 1:7
HeartAttacks
Psalm 55:4
Luke 21:26
John 14:27;
14:1
Torment—
Horror
Psalm 55:5
1 John 4:18
Fear of Satan
& His
Demons

Nightmares –
Terrors
Psalm 91:5,6
Isaiah 54:14
Fear of
Persecution/Confrontation
Fear of Rejection, Fear
Of Saying No
Fear of Man
Proverbs 29:25
Jeremiah 1:8;17-19

Ezekiel 2:6,7; 3:9
Fear of Death/Dying
Psalm 45:4
Hebrews 2:14,15
Panic Attacks

Anxiety – Stress
1 Peter 5:7
Fear of Mental Imbalance
& Incompetence
Untrusting – Doubt
Matthew 8:26
Revelation 21:8
Fear of Criticism, Fear of
Failing, Suspicion &
Distrust
Fear of Being an
Introvert
Fear That Brings Mental
Confusion & a Double
Mind
Physical Illnesses &
Pains

And I cast you out of me, __________, __________, __________, and everybody I have prayed for today along with all of your works, roots, fruits, tentacles, links and spirits, and I loose you from us and I force you into outer darkness in the Name of Jesus Christ.

I bind you in the Name of Jesus Christ and declare that all of your works, roots, fruits, tentacles, links, and spirits, are dead works in my life ___________, ___________, ___________, ___________, and the lives of everybody I have prayed for today, in Jesus Christ' Name, and I bind you and loose you from me, everybody I have prayed for today and I loose you to go wherever Jesus Christ sends you and command you not to come back into our presence again. I ask You, Heavenly Father, to loose into me and each person I have prayed for today the Power, Love and A Sound Mind according to 2 Timothy 1:7 Amen.

Bind: Spirit of Fear

Loose: Power. Love and A Sound Mind

2 Timothy 1:7

Spirit of Leviathan

Proverbs 6:16-19

"Strongman called Spirit of Leviathan, I bind you in the Name of Jesus Christ along with all of your works, roots, fruits, tentacles, links and spirits that are in my life ___________, ___________, ___________, ___________, and the lives of everybody I have prayed for today, along with all of your fruits and spirits of:

Arrogant-Smug
2 Samuel 22:8
Jeremiah 48:29
Isaiah 2:1 1,17; 5:15
Pride
Proverbs 6:16,17; 16:18,19;
28:25
Isaiah 16:6
Idleness
Ezekiel 16:49,50
Scornful
Proverbs 1:22; 3:34;
21:24; 24:9; 29:8
Strife
Proverbs 28:25
Obstinate/Stubborn
Proverbs 29:1
Daniel 5:20

Contentious
Proverbs 13:10
Self-Deception
Jeremiah 49: 16
Obadiah 1:3
Self-Righteous
Luke 18:11,12
Rejection of God
Psalm 10:4

Jeremiah 43:2
Critical, Fault Finding
Rebellion
1 Samuel 15:23
Proverbs 29:1
Contempt, Mocking
Judgmental
Interrupting spirit
Haughtiness

And I cast you out of me __________, __________, __________, and everybody I have prayed for today along with all of your works, roots, fruits, tentacles, links and spirits, and I loose you from us and I force you into outer darkness in the Name of Jesus Christ.

I bind you in the Name of Jesus Christ and declare that all of your works, roots, fruits, tentacles, links, and spirits, are dead works in my life __________, __________, __________, __________, and the lives of everybody I have prayed for today, in Jesus Christ' Name, and I bind you and loose you from me, everybody I have prayed for today and I loose you to go wherever Jesus Christ sends you and command you not to come back into our presence again. I ask You, Heavenly Father, to loose into me and each person I have prayed for today A Humble and Contrite Spirit according to Proverbs 16, 19 and Romans 1:4. Amen
Bind: Spirit of Leviathan
Loose: A Humble and Contrite Spirit
Proverbs 6:16-19: Romans 1:4

Spirit of Heaviness

Isaiah 61:3

"Strongman called Spirit of Heaviness, I bind you in the Name of Jesus Christ along with all of your works, roots, fruits, tentacles, links and spirits that are in my life __________, __________, __________, __________, and the lives of everybody I have prayed for today, along with all of your fruits and spirits of:

Excessive Mourning
Isaiah 61:3
Luke 4:18
Sorrow—Grief
Nehemiah 2:2
Proverbs 15:13
Insomnia
Jeremiah 2:2
Broken-Heart
Psalm 69:20
Proverbs 12:18; 15:3,13; 18:14
Luke 4:18
Self-Pity
Psalm 69:20
Rejection
Depression
Isaiah 61:3

Despair-Dejection
Hopelessness
2 Corinthians 1:8,9
Withdrawing/Pouting
Excessive Fatigue & Weariness
Suicidal Thoughts
Mark 9
Inner Hurts-Torn Spirit

Luke 4:18
Proverbs 18:14; 26:22
Heaviness
Isaiah 61:3
Escape/Indifference;
Root of Bitterness
Sadness, Abandonment.
Loneliness
Suppressed Emotions
Physical Illnesses & Pains

And I cast you out of me ___________, ___________, ___________, and everybody I have prayed for today along with all of your works, roots, fruits, tentacles, links and spirits, and I loose you from us and I force you into outer darkness in the Name of Jesus Christ.

I bind you in the Name of Jesus Christ and declare that all of your works, roots, fruits, tentacles, links, and spirits, are dead works in my life ___________, ___________, ___________, ___________, and the lives of everybody I have prayed for today, in Jesus Christ' Name, and I bind you and loose you form me, everybody I have prayed for today and I loose you to go wherever Jesus Christ sends you and command you not to come back into our presence again. Heavenly Father, I loose into me and each person I the Comforter, Garment of Praise, The Oil of Joy according to John 15:26; Isaiah 61:3. Amen
Bind: Spirit of Heaviness
Loose: Comforter. Garment of Praise, The Oil of Joy
John 15:26; Isaiah 61:3

Spirit of Infirmity

Luke 13:11-13

"Strongman called Spirit of Infirmity, I bind you in the Name of Jesus Christ along with all of your works, roots, fruits, tentacles, links and spirits that are in my life __________, __________, __________, __________, and the lives of everybody I have prayed for today, along with all of your fruits and spirits of:

Bent Body—Spine
Luke 13:11

Impotent – Frail – Lame
John 5:5
Acts 3:2; Acts 4:9

Migraine Headaches
Asthma – Hay Fever –
Allergies
John 5:5

Arthritis
John 5:5

Weakness
Luke 13:11
John 5:5

Oppression
Acts 10:38

Fevers

Physical Illnesses & Pains
Lingering Disorders
Luke 13:11
John 5:5

Cancer
Luke 13:11
John 5:4

And I cast you out of me __________, __________, __________, and everybody I have prayed for today along with all of your works, roots, fruits, tentacles, links and spirits, and I loose you from us and I force you into outer darkness in the Name of Jesus Christ.

I bind you in the Name of Jesus Christ and declare that all of your works, roots, fruits, tentacles, links, and spirits, are dead works in my life __________, __________, __________, __________, and the lives of everybody I have prayed for today, in Jesus Christ' Name, and I bind you and loose you from me, everybody I have prayed for today and I loose you to go wherever Jesus Christ sends you and command you not to come back into our presence again. I ask You, Heavenly Father, to loose into me and each person I have prayed for today the Spirit of Life and His Gifts of Healing according to Romans 8:2 and 1 Corinthians 12:9 Amen
Bind: Spirit of Infirmity
Loose: Spirit of Life and His Gifts of Healing
Romans 8:2; 1 Corinthians 12:9-12

Spirit of Jealousy

Numbers 5:14

"Strongman called Spirit of Jealousy, I bind you in the Name of Jesus Christ along with all of your works, roots, fruits, tentacles, links and spirits that are in my life ___________, ___________, ___________, ___________, and the lives of everybody I have prayed for today, along with all of your fruits and spirits of:

Murder
Genesis 4:8
Revenge—Spite
Proverbs 6:34
Proverbs 14:16,17
Anger-Rage
Genesis 4:5,6
Proverbs 6:34; 14:29
22:24,25; 29:22,23
Jealousy
Numbers 5:14,30
Cruelty
Song of Solomon 8:6
Proverbs 27:4
Strife
Proverbs 10:12

Hatred
Genesis 37:3, 4,8
1 Thessalonians 4:8
Extreme Competition
Genesis 4:4,5
Bitterness, Resentment
Contention
Proverbs 13:10
Spirit That Causes Divisions/
Divorce
Galatians 5:19

Envy
Proverbs 14:30
Prejudice/Bigotry
Violence/Retaliation
Suspicion/Distrust
Unforgiveness

And I cast you out of me ___________, ___________, ___________, And everybody I have prayed for today along with all of your works, roots, fruits, tentacles, links and spirits, and I loose you from us and I force you into outer darkness in the Name of Jesus Christ.

I bind you in the Name of Jesus Christ and declare that all of your works, roots, fruits, tentacles, links, and spirits, are dead works in my life ___________, ___________, ___________, ___________, and the lives of everybody I have prayed for today, in Jesus Christ' Name, and I bind you and loose you from me, everybody I have prayed for today and I loose you to go wherever Jesus Christ sends you and command you not to come back into our presence again. I ask You, Heavenly Father, to loose into me and each person I have prayed for today the Love of God according to 1 Corinthians 13 Ephesians 5:2. Amen
Bind: Spirit of Jealousy
Loose: Love of God
1 Corinthians 13; Ephesians 5:2

Lying Spirit

2 Chronicles 18:22

"Strongman called Lying Spirit I bind you in the Name of Jesus Christ along with all of your works, roots, fruits, tentacles, links and spirits that are in my life __________, __________, __________, __________, and the lives of everybody I have prayed for today, along with all of your fruits and spirits of:

Strong Deception
2 Thessalonians 2:9-13
Flattery
Psalms 78:36
Proverbs 20:19; 26:28; 29:5
Superstitions
1 Timothy 4:7
Profanity
Religious Bondages
Galatians 5:1
False Prophecy
Jeremiah 23:16-17; 27:9,10
Matthew 7:15
Accusations
Revelation 12:10
Psalms 21:18

Slander
Proverbs 6:16-19
Gossip
1 Timothy 6:20
2 Timothy 2:16
Homosexuality
Romans 1:27
Lies
2 Chronicles 18:22
Proverbs 6:16:19

False Teachers
2 Peter (Whole Book)
Driving Zeal
Guilt/Shame, Condemnation
Extortion
Exaggeration
Foolish Talking

And I cast you out of me ___________, ___________, ___________, and everybody I have prayed for today along with all of your works, roots, fruits, tentacles, links and spirits, and I loose you from us and I force you into outer darkness in the Name of Jesus Christ.

I bind you in the Name of Jesus Christ and declare that all of your works, roots, fruits, tentacles, links, and spirits, are dead works in my life ___________, ___________, ___________, ___________, and the lives of everybody 1prayed for today, in Jesus Christ' Name, and I bind you and loose you from me, everybody I prayed for today and I loose you to go wherever Jesus Christ sends you and command you not to come back into our presence again. I ask You, Heavenly Father, to loose into me and each person I have prayed for today the Spirit of Truth according to John 14:17, 16:13,26. Amen
Bind: Lying Spirit
Loose: Spirit of Truth
John 14:17; 16:13,26

Perverse Spirit

Isaiah 19:14

"Strongman called Perverse Spirit, I bind you in the Name of Jesus Christ along with all of your works, roots, fruits, tentacles, links and spirits that are in my life __________, __________, __________, __________, and the lives of everybody I have prayed for today, along with all of your fruits and spirits of:

Evil Actions
Proverbs 17:20,23
Broken Spirit
Proverbs 15:14
Atheist
Proverbs 14:2
Romans 1:30
Abortion
Exodus 20:13; 21,22,25
Child Abuse, Incest, Rape
Molestation, Pedophilia
Filthy Mind
Proverbs 2:12; 23:33
Doctrinal Error
Isaiah 19:14
Romans 1:22,23
2 Timothy 3:7,8
Sex Perversions
Romans 1:17-322
2 Timothy 3:2

Foolish
Proverbs 1:2; 19:1
Twisting the Word of God
Acts 13:10
2 Peter 2:14
Incubus/Secubus
Frigidity, Prostitution,

Bestiality, Sodomy, Oral Sex,
Homosexuality, Lesbianism,
Masturbation, Exhibitionist
Contentions
Philippians 2:14-16
1 Timothy 6:4,5
Titus 3:10,11
Lust & Pornography
Unholy spirit, Ungodliness,
Heresies
Chronic Worrier
Proverbs 19:33
Sadism-Masochism

And I cast you out of me ___________, ___________, ___________, And everybody I have prayed for today along with all of your works, roots, fruits, tentacles, links and spirits, and I loose you from us and I force you into outer darkness in the Name of Jesus Christ.

I bind you in the Name of Jesus Christ and declare that all of your works, roots, fruits, tentacles, links, and spirits, are dead works in my life ___________, ___________, ___________, ___________, and the lives of everybody I have prayed for today, in Jesus Christ' Name, and I bind you and loose you from me, everybody I have prayed for today and I loose you to go wherever Jesus Christ sends you and command you not to come back into our presence again. I ask You, Heavenly Father, to loose into me and each person I have prayed for today God's Spirit of Pureness and Holiness according to Zechariah 12:10 and Hebrews 10:29. Amen
Bind: Perverse Spirit
Loose: God's Spirit of Pureness and Holiness
Zechariah 12:10; Hebrews 10:29

Spirit of Whoredoms

Hosea 5:4

"Strongman called Spirit of Whoredoms, I bind you in the Name of Jesus Christ along with all of your works, roots, fruits, tentacles, links and spirits that are in my life __________, __________, __________, __________, and the lives of everyone I have prayed for today, along with all of your fruits and spirits of:

Unfaithfulness/Adultery
Ezekiel 16:15,28
Proverbs 5:1-4
Galatians 5:19
Spirit, Soul or Body
Prostitution
Ezekiel 16:15,28
Deuteronomy 23: 17, 18
Chronic Dissatisfaction
Ezekiel 16:28
Idolatry
Judges 2:17
Ezekiel 1:6
Leviticus 17:7

Love of Money
Proverbs 15:27
1 Timothy 6:7-14
Excessive Appetite
Gluttony
Corinthians 6:13-16
Philippians 3:19
Fornication
Hosea4:13-19
Worldliness
James 4:4
Stealing

Break All Soul Ties
Genesis 2:24;
1 Corinthians 6:16
Rock & Country Music

And I cast you out of me ___________, ___________, ___________, and everybody I have prayed for today along with all of your works, roots, fruits, tentacles, links and spirits, and I loose you from us and I force you into outer darkness in the Name of Jesus Christ.

I bind you in the Name of Jesus Christ and declare that all of your works, roots, fruits, tentacles, links, and spirits, are dead works in my life ___________, ___________, ___________, ___________, and the lives of everybody I have prayed for today, in Jesus Christ' Name, and I bind you and loose you from me, everybody I have prayed for today and I loose you to go wherever Jesus Christ sends you and command you not to come back into our presence again. I ask You, Heavenly Father, to loose into me and each person I have prayed for today the Spirit of God, a Pure Spirit according to Ephesians 3:16. Amen
Bind: Spirit of Whoredoms
Loose: Spirit of God, A Pure Spirit
Ephesians 3:16

Spiritual Warfare Prayer

Heavenly Father, I (we) come to You now in the Name of my (our) Lord and Savior Christ Jesus.

(Note—if two or more praying) Heavenly Father, _____ and I come to You in one accord in the Name of Christ Jesus of Nazareth. We come two or more in agreement touching heaven and earth and You said it will be done, so, according to Matthew 18:19, we ask You to do the following in the Name of Jesus Christ of Nazareth.)

Heavenly Father, I (we) pray for _____, _____, _____, and _____ and ask You to forgive me (us) for all of our sins, iniquities, trespasses, transgressions, sins of commission, sins of omission and specifically any sins of: _____, _____, _____ and any unknown sins according to Psalms 19:12. Cover them with the Blood of the Lord Christ Jesus, and cleanse me (us) of all unrighteousness according to Your Word, 1 John 1:9 and John 14:14, in Christ Jesus' Holy Name, I (we) ask you to do this.

Heavenly Father, I (we) thank You *that no weapon formed against us shall prosper.* I (we) thank You *that every tongue and every word that rises against me (us) in judgment; You shall condemn.* I (we) thank You Heavenly Father *that this* is *the heritage of the servants of the Lord, and our righteousness is from You* according to Isaiah 54:17.

Heavenly Father, I (we) thank You that it is written "*For the weapons of our warfare are not carnal, but mighty through God to the pulling down of strongholds; Casting down imaginations, and every high thing that exalteth itself against the knowledge of God, and bringing into captivity every thought to the obedience of Christ* according to 2Corinthians 10:4-5.

Heavenly Father, in the Name of Christ Jesus, I (we) pull down every demonic stronghold (name them if you know them—doubt, confusion, etc.) that I (we) have in my (our) mind or in the minds of anyone that I (we) have prayed for today. I (we) pull down and cast them aside in the Name of the Lord Christ Jesus. I (we) pull down every vain imagination in me (us) and every vain imagination in everyone that I (we) have prayed for today. I (we) pull them down and cast them aside in the Name of the Lord Christ Jesus. I (we) pull down every high thought in me (us) and every high thought in everyone that I (we) have prayed for today that exalts itself against the knowledge of God. I (we) pull them down and cast them aside in the Name of the Lord Jesus Christ of Nazareth and I (we) bring every thought captive in each of us to the obedience of Christ Jesus according to 1 Corinthians 10:3-6. Lord Jesus; I (we) thank You that "*the yoke will be destroyed because of the anointing oil,*" according to Isaiah 10:27. Heavenly Father, I (we) ask You now to cause Your anointing to break and destroy any yokes of bondage including _____, (name them if you know them-example: fear, doubt, lust, drug abuse, sexual impurity, etc.); along with all of their works, roots, fruits, tentacles and links that are in my (our) life (lives), and the lives of anyone that I (we) have prayed for today.

Heavenly Father, I (we) ask You to give us deliverance and freedom from all these bondages in the Name of Christ Jesus according to John 16:23.

Heavenly Father, I (we) ask You according to John 14:14, to loose Your angels in great abundance in my (our) presence, the presence of everyone that I (we) have prayed for today and into our homes, cars, trucks, lands, properties, buildings, and work places, in great abundance, to protect us, guard us and to force out, drive out, and cleanse out all evil, wicked demon and tormenting spirits from our presence, and our homes, cars, trucks, lands, properties, animals, and work places and send them to where Christ Jesus sends them, in Christ Jesus' Holy Name.

Heavenly Father, I (we) pray Psalms 35:1-6 over myself (ourselves), __________, and __________. "*Plead our cause,*

O Lord, with them that strive with us, fight against those that fight against us. Take hold of shield and buckler and stand up for our help! Also draw out the spear and stop those who pursue us. Say to our souls, "I am your salvation." Let those be put to shame and brought to dishonor who seek after our lives. Let those be turned back and brought to confusion who plot our hurt. Let them be chaff before the wind, and let the angels of the Lord chase them. Let their way be dark and slippery. Let the angels of the Lord pursue them. For without cause they have hidden their net for me (us) in a pit, which they have dug without cause for my (our) life. Let destruction come upon him unexpectedly, and let his net that he has hidden catch himself; into that very destruction let him fall" according to Psalms 35:1-8.

Heavenly Father, Hear my (our) cry, O God; Attend to my (our) prayer. From the end of the earth I (we) will cry unto You, when my (our) heart is overwhelmed; Lead me (us) to the rock that is higher than I (us). For You have been a shelter for me, A strong tower from the enemy. I (we) will abide in Your tabernacle forever; I (we) will trust in the shelter of Your wings. For You, O God, have heard my (our) vows; You have given me (us) the heritage of those who fear Your Name. I (we) ask You to let me (us) abide with You forever and prepare mercy and truth, which may preserve me (us). So we will sing praise to Your Name forever, that I (we) may daily perform my (our) vows according to Psalms 61.

Heavenly Father, hear my (our) voice, O God, in my (our) meditation; Preserve my (our) life from fear of the enemy. Hide me (us) from the secret plots of the wicked, from the rebellion of the workers of iniquity, who sharpen their tongue like a sword, and bend their bows to shoot their arrows – bitter words at me (us). I (we) ask You, Heavenly Father to shoot at them with an arrow; suddenly wound them and make them stumble over their own tongue; all who see them shall flee away, all men shall fear, and shall declare the work of God; for they will wisely consider Your doing. The righteous shall be glad in the Lord, and trust in Him. And all the upright in heart shall glory according to Psalms 64.

Heavenly Father, in You, O Lord, I (we) put my (our) trust; Let me (us) never be ashamed; Deliver me (us) in Your righteousness. Bow down Your ear to me (us), deliver me (us) speedily; Be my (our) rock of refuge, a fortress of defense to save me (us). For You are my (our) rock and my (our) fortress; Therefore, for Your Name's sake, lead me (us) and guide me (us). Pull me (us) out of the net that they have secretly laid for me (us). For You are my (our) strength. Into Your hand I (we) commit my (our) spirit; Redeem me (us), O Lord God of truth. I (we) have hated those who regard useless idols; but I (we) trust in You, Heavenly Father. I (we) will be glad and rejoice in Your mercy, for You have considered my (our) trouble; You have known my (our) soul in adversities, and You have not shut me (us) up into the hand of the enemy; You have set my (our) feet in a wide place. Have mercy on me (us), O Lord, for I am (we are) in trouble according to Psalms 31:1-9.

Heavenly Father, we thank You that it is written in Psalms 32; Blessed is he whose transgression is forgiven, whose sin is covered. Blessed is the man to whom the Lord does not impute iniquity, and in whose spirit there is no deceit. I (we) have acknowledged my (our) sin to You, and my (our) iniquity I (we) have not hidden. I (we) said, "I (we) will confess my (our) transgressions to the Lord," and You forgave the iniquity of my (our) sin. For this cause everyone who is godly shall pray to You in a time when You may be found; surely in a flood of great waters they shall not come near me (us). You are my (our) hiding place; You shall preserve me (us) from trouble; You shall surround me (us) with songs of deliverance. I (we) thank You for instructing and teaching me (us) in the way I (we) should go and guiding me (us) with Your eyes according to Psalms 32:1-8. Heavenly Father, I (we) thank You "For when the enemy shall come in, like a flood Your Holy Spirit will lift up a standard against him", according to Isaiah 59:19. Heavenly Father, I (we) ask You to nullify, dismantle, cancel and stop all works of darkness which are designed to hinder, prevent, deny, or delay Your original plans and purposes for our lives according to Daniel 7:25. Lord Christ Jesus, thank You for redeeming us from the curse according to Galatians 3:13; "Christ has redeemed us from the curse of the law, having become a curse for us". Heavenly Father, thank you for saving me (us) and all members of our household (s) according to Acts 16:31; "Believe on the Lord Jesus Christ, and you will be saved, you and your household."

Hedge of Protection Prayer

Heavenly Father, I (we) ask You to execute divine judgment against satanic/demonic activities and help us war in the spirit of Elijah and Jehu according to I Kings 18:1-46, 9-10:2. In the Name of the Lord Jesus Christ of Nazareth, I (we) bind all of satan's evil, wicked, demon, lying and tormenting spirits and strongmen along with all their works, roots, fruits, tentacles, and links of: ______, ______ (say what applies—examples: addictions, bad language, conniving, discouragements, fears, lusts, insomnia, pride, stress, willful sins, withdrawal, worries) all spirits and strongmen of all mental, physical, and emotional illness, sickness, diseases, disorders, death, premature death, infirmities, afflictions, inflammations, viruses, infections, abnormal cells, radical cells, lesions, cysts, pains, shock, trauma, spasms, cramps, abnormal growths, radical growths, in or on any parts of our bodies, including our eyes, ears, nose, mouth, throat, back, bones, muscles, ligaments, tissues, blood, blood vessels, arteries, colons, intestines, stomach, prostate, thyroid, brain, liver, heart, lungs, cardiovascular disorders and diseases, reproductive disorders and diseases, thyroid disorders and diseases, blood pressure disorders and diseases, throat disorders and diseases, breast disorders and diseases, neurological disorders and diseases, lymphatic disorders and diseases, chemical imbalances, hormone imbalances, allergies of any kind, senility, forgetfulness, paranoia, schizophrenia, all spirits of arthritis, crippling arthritis, acute arthritis, sinusitis, acute sinusitis, performance spirits, all spirits of disorders and diseases, hypoglycemia of all forms, degenerative diseases of all kinds, and all cancers, all tumors, and all mind diseases and disorders. I bind and loose all these demonic spirits and strongmen from me (us), from everyone that I (we) have prayed for today, along with all evil principalities, powers, and rulers of wickedness in high places, from every organ in our bodies, from every cell in our bodies, from every gland in our bodies, from our homes, properties, marriages, cars, trucks, businesses, ministries, objects, work places, finances, etc., and I (we) loose them to go where Jesus sends them and I (we) bind them and command them to stay there in the Name of Jesus Christ of Nazareth. I (we) place the Blood of the Lord Christ Jesus between us.

Heavenly Father, I (we) ask You to destroy all demonic covenants, contracts, chains, fetters, bondages, proclivities and captivities that are contrary to, oppose, or hinder Your Will and destiny for our lives. I (we) ask that You liberate me (us) from generational, satanic, and/or demonic alliances, allegiances, soul ties, spirits of inheritances and curses. Free us from any and all influences passed down from one generation to another; biologically, socially, emotionally, psychologically, spiritually, or any other channel unknown to me, but known to You. I (we) resist every spirit that acts as a gatekeeper or doorkeeper to my (our) soul, and renounce any further conscious or unconscious alliance, association, allegiance, or covenant. I (we) open us to divine deliverance. Heavenly Father, have Your way now! Perfect those things concerning us. I (we) ask these things in the Name of the Lord Jesus Christ according to John 12:14. Lord Jesus, I (we) ask You to destroy all ill spoken words, all ill wishes, all enchantments, all spells, hexes, curses, all witchcraft prayers, psychic prayers, witchcraft spells, voodoo spells, satanic spells, and every idle word spoken contrary to God's original plans and purposes. Lord Jesus, I (we) ask that You destroy the curses associated with these utterances and decree and declare that: they shall not stand; they shall not come to pass; they shall not take root; and their violent verbal dealings are returned to them double-fold according to Isaiah 54:17.

Heavenly Father, I (we) ask You to place a hedge of protection around me (us). It hides me (us) from the enemy, familiar spirits, any and all demon spirits, making it difficult, if not impossible for them to effectively track or trace me in the realm of the spirit. There shall be no perforations or penetrations to these hedges of protection according to Job 1:7-10, Psalms 91:1-16, Exodus 12:13, and Zechariah 2:5.

Heavenly Father, I (we) ask You to place our names on the hearts of all prayer warriors, intercessors, and prophetic watchmen who will pray for me (us). I (we) ask You to let them not cease or come down from their watchtowers until their assignments have been completed. Heavenly Father, I (we) ask that they will conduct their intercessory assignments under the direction of the Holy Spirit and Christ Jesus who is my (our) chief intercessor according to Jeremiah 27:18, Ezekiel 3:17, and John 16:13. Heavenly Father, I (we) declare that our times and seasons are in the hands of the Lord and they shall not be altered or adjusted by anyone or anything. We function under Your anointing and You give us the divine ability to accurately discern our times and seasons according to 1 Chronicles 12:32, Psalms 31:15, Ecclesiastes 3:1-8, and Daniel 2:21-22.

Heavenly Father, I (we) declare that from this day forward we will operate according to Your divine timetable/calendar. I (we) declare that Your agenda is my (our) agenda. We are not our own, we have been bought with a price. I (we) therefore submit to You alone. I (we) bind our minds to the mind of Christ. I bind our wills to the Will of God. I (we) declare that "I come: in the volume of the book it is written of me" according to Psalms 40:7, 139:16, 1 Corinthians 7:23, and James 4:7.

Lord Jesus, I (we) bring all my (our) burdens and lay them at the foot of Your cross, especially the burdens of ________, ________, ________, and ________. I (we) ask You to manage all areas of our lives. I (we) totally rely on You, Christ Jesus, to take care of us, our families, our health, and our finances. Heavenly Father, I ask that Your Will be done in our lives. Heavenly Father, I (we) declare "that at the Name of Jesus every knee should bow, of things in heaven, and things in the earth, and things under the earth; And that every tongue should confess that Jesus Christ is Lord, to the glory of You, God the Father" according to Philippians 2:10-11. Heavenly Father, I (we) ask You to prohibit the accuser of the brethren from operating or influencing the soul or mind of anyone who comes into contact with us according to Revelation 12:10. I (we) declare that divine favor, grace, honor, ·and well-wishes now replace any and all negative feelings, perceptions, and thoughts concerning us, our families, our work, and our ministries which we are called to accomplish. I (we) declare that nobility and greatness is our portion according to Genesis 12:1-3 and Psalms 5:12. Heavenly Father, You have called us to do great works for You. I (we) ask You to release all finances and all resources that belong to us. I (we) ask You to release everything prepared for us before the foundation of the world that pertains to our lives, our ministries, our calling. We shall not, we will not be denied! We shall not, and we will not accept substitutes. In the Name of Christ Jesus, I (we) declare that every resource necessary for me (us) to fulfill God's original plans and purposes comes to us without delay according to 2 Peter 1-3. Almighty God, In the Name of Christ Jesus grant unto us, according to Your riches in glory, Your tender mercies and immeasurable favor, the treasures of darkness and hidden riches of secret places according to Isaiah 45:1-3. I (we) declare that the Cyrus anointing flows unhindered and uncontaminated in our lives according to Isaiah 60:10-17, and Philippians 4:19. Lift up your heads, oh ye gates; and be lifted up forever, you abiding doors that the King of Glory, the Lord strong and mighty, the Lord of Hosts, may come in according to Psalms 24:7-10. Therefore, we will not and cannot be denied of what rightfully belongs to us! Heavenly Father, I (we) declare that the laws that govern this prayer and all spiritual warfare strategies and tactics, are binding by the Word, the Blood, and by the Holy Spirit according to I John 5:7-8. Heavenly Father, I (we) thank You that it is written in Isaiah 53:5 "But He was wounded for our transgressions, He was bruised for our iniquities: the chastisement of our peace was upon Him: and with His stripes we are healed." I (we) thank You for healing us. Heavenly Father, I (we) praise

You and thank You for strengthening the bars of my (our) gates; for blessing my (our) children, and making peace in my (our) borders according to Psalms 147:12-14. Heavenly Father, I (we) place upon us: the armor of light; and the Lord Jesus Christ according to Romans 13:12, 14. Heavenly Father, in Jesus' Holy Name, I (we) place upon us the belt of truth, the breastplate of righteousness, the gospel of peace sandals, the shield of faith to quench the fiery darts of the enemy, the helmet of salvation, the sword of the Spirit, which is the Word of God according to Ephesians 6:13-17. Heavenly Father, if You have made a decision to take us home before the next rapture, I ask You to give us an extension of our lives according to John 16:23, as You did for Hezekiah according to Isaiah 38:1-5, or until Jesus comes to get us in the next rapture. Heavenly Father, I (we) declare that "we are a chosen generation, a royal priesthood, a holy nation, a peculiar people: that we shall show forth the praises of Christ Jesus who has called us out of darkness into His marvelous light" according to 1 Peter 2:9. Heavenly Father, I (we) thank You for Your promise: "I will make you a great nation; I will bless you and make your name great; and you shall be a blessing. I will bless those who bless you, and I will curse him who curses you; and in you all the families of the earth shall be blessed.", according to Genesis 12:2-3.

Heavenly Father, I (we) pray that You, almighty God, will bless us, and make us fruitful and multiply us. That we may be an assembly of peoples; and give us the blessing of Abraham, to us and our descendants with us, that we may inherit the land in which we are a stranger, which God gave to Abraham according to Genesis 28:3-4. Heavenly Father, I (we) pray that You would bless us indeed, and enlarge our territory, and that Your hand will be with us, and that You would keep us from evil, that we may cause no pain! Heavenly Father, I thank You for granting us this request according to 1 Chronicles 4:10. Heavenly Father, I (we) ask You to bless us when we come in. I (we) ask You to bless us when we go out. I (we) ask You to bless us in the city. I (we) ask You to bless us in the country. I (we) ask You to bless our fruits.

I (we) ask You to bless our seed. I (we) ask You to bless our land. I (we) ask You to bless our storehouse. I (we) ask You to bless and prosper everything we touch. I (we) ask You to cause our enemies to come in one direction but to flee in seven directions because greater is You, Who is in us, than he that is in the world. Heavenly Father, I (we) thank You for Your blessings and I (we) pray them over me (us) and everyone we have prayed for today according to Psalms 115:14-16. "He will bless us that fear the Lord, both small and great. The Lord shall increase us more and more, us and our children. We are blessed of the Lord which made heaven and earth. The heaven, even the heavens, are the Lord's: but the earth hath He given to the children of men." Heavenly Father, thank You for continually increasing our anointing, our love for one another other, our health, and our finances. Heavenly Father, in Christ Jesus' Holy Name I (we) thank You for Your Word in Numbers 6:23-26. Heavenly Father, I (we) pray that You will bless me (us), everyone that I (we) have prayed for today and that You will keep us. I pray that You will make Your face shine upon me (us), and be gracious to us. I pray that You will lift up Your countenance upon me (us) and give us peace. Heavenly Father, (we) thank You for blessing us! Heavenly Father, I (we) thank You for releasing Your angels to fulfill the blessings we speak. "Bless the Lord, ye His angels, that excel in strength, that do His commandments, hearkening unto the Voice of His Word.", according to Psalms 103:20.

Bless the Lord! Bless the Lord, oh my (our) soul, and all that is within me (us), bless His Holy Name. Bless the Lord, oh my (our) soul, and forget not all of His benefits, who forgives all my (our) iniquities; who heals all my (our) diseases, Who redeems my (our) life from destruction, Who crowns me (us) with loving kindness and tender mercies, Who gives me (us) good things to eat, so that my (our) youth is renewed like the eagle's, and has pity on me (us) and I (we) thank You that the angels harkens to the Voice of Your Word according to Psalms 103:1-3, 13, 20. Blessed are You, Lord God of Israel, our Father, forever and ever. Yours, O Lord, is the greatness, the power and the glory, the victory and the majesty; for all that is in heaven and in earth is Yours; Yours is the kingdom, O Lord, and You are exalted as head over all. Both riches and honor come from You, and You reign over all. In Your hand is power and might; In Your hand it is to make great and to give strength to all, according to 1 Chronicles 29:10-12 Lord Jesus, I (we) ask you to do all of these things according to John 14:14; and Heavenly Father, I (we) ask You to give us these things according to John 16:23. In the Name of the Lord Jesus Christ of Nazareth, I (we) pray with thanksgiving. Amen.

Communion Prayer

Heavenly Father, I (we) come to You now in the Name of my (our) Lord and Savior Christ Jesus.

Heavenly Father, I (we) thank You that we can enter in communion at this time. We thank You that Your Word says in 1 Corinthians 11:27, that "Whoever shall eat of the Bread of Life and drink of the Cup of the Lord, in an unworthy manner shall be guilty of the Body and the Blood of Jesus Christ." Your Word says let every man examine himself, so let each of us examine ourselves now (pause). Heavenly Father, I (we) ask You to forgive me (us), _____, and _____, of our sins, transgressions, iniquities, and our trespasses, cover each of us with the Blood of Jesus Christ and cleanse us each of all unrighteousness. Heavenly Father, I (we) thank You that we are now able to enter into communion with You at this time. I (We) thank You that the Lord Jesus Christ went to the cross for us, that Jesus took my sins, my transgressions, our iniquities, and our trespasses to the cross with Him. I (We) thank You that we can take this piece of bread (body) in remembrance of Jesus. We thank You Lord Jesus that Your body was broken for our sins, our transgressions, our iniquities, and our trespasses. Lord Jesus, we love You. We remember Your suffering, and how You were beaten and marred, spit upon, whipped and crucified for each of us. Your body was broken so that our body may be healed. I (we) thank You that with Your stripes we are healed in the Name of the Lord Jesus. Dear Jesus, thank You for loving us, touching us, and healing us. We thank You that You took the bread and broke it and said take, eat, this is my body which was broken for you and partake in faith in the Name of Jesus. Dear Jesus, we now take this piece of bread (your body) in remembrance of You in faith. Your Word says in 1 Corinthians, that after supper, Jesus took the cup and said this to His disciples: "This is the Blood of the new testament shed for you." We thank You Lord Jesus that You shed Your Blood for us, that Your Blood is our atonement. It justifies us, sanctifies us, redeems us and cleanses and washes away all our sins, all of our iniquities, all of our transgressions, all of our trespasses and Your Blood heals us in the Name of Jesus. I (we) now take this in remembrance of You. In the Name of Jesus Christ of Nazareth, we pray with thanksgiving. Amen!

Destroying Generational Curses

Heavenly Father, I (we) come to You now in the Name of my (our) Lord and Savior Christ Jesus. Lord Jesus Christ, I (we) believe that You are the Son of God; that You died on the cross for my (our) sins; that God raised You from the dead and You ascended to heaven. Heavenly Father, I (we) repent of any sins in my (our) life (lives) and my (our) ancestors' lives, going back 25 generations, that have resulted in a curse or curses on me, or on _____. I (we) repent of all and any sins of: not keeping Your commandments: having other gods before You; making or buying images, bowing down to or serving images; for taking the Lord my (our) God's Name in vain; for not observing and keeping holy the Sabbath day; not honoring my (our) father and/or mother; murder; adultery; stealing; bearing false witness; coveting a neighbor's spouse, house, land, servants, donkey, or anything that is my neighbor's; not loving You with all my heart, with all my soul, and with all my mind; not loving my neighbor as myself, or not loving myself (see sin list). I (we) ask Your forgiveness and cleansing through the Blood of the Lord Jesus Christ according to 1 John 1:9 and John 14:14. Heavenly Father, I (we) repented of all of my (our) sins and I (we) thank You for forgiving me (us). In the Name of the Lord Jesus Christ, I (we) now ask You to destroy all curses, generational curses that have been placed on me (us), my (our) spouse, and my (our) children, including ten generations.

Bondage Breaking Prayer

Lord Jesus, Your Word says that Your anointing breaks and destroys all yokes of bondage so I (we) ask You now to cause Your anointing to break and destroy any yokes of bondages; along with all their works, roots, fruits, tentacles, and links, in the Name of Jesus Christ of Nazareth (Say what applies to you). (Partial List: deception, desires of this world, disbelief, disdain, disobedience, dissension, division, divination, doubt, egoism, envy, false burdens, fantasy lust, fears, fornication, fretting, giving offense, gossip, greed, guilt, hard-heartedness, heaviness, hate, haughtiness, hypocrisy, idolatry, impatience, indifferences, intimidation, intolerance, irritation, jealousy, being judgmental, laboring, lasciviousness, legalism, lust, lust of the eye, lust of the flesh, lust of the mind, lying, manipulation, misbelief, murder, plotting, presumption, pride, provoking, railing, rebellion, resentment, restlessness, rigidity, rudeness, sexual idolatry, sexual immorality, sexual impurity, sexual perversion, selfishness, self-centeredness, self-delusion, self-confusion, self-righteousness, self-condemnation, self-criticalness, self-analysis, self-deception, self-pity, sodomy, strife, shame, slander, stiff-necked, struggling, taking offense, tension, unbelief, uncleanliness, undermining, unforgiveness, unsubmissiveness, vanity, worry, worldliness, wickedness, witchcraft, mischief, perfectionism, oppression, depression, frustrations, addictions, dependencies, murmuring, complaining, petulance, all unrighteousness, sin consciousness, demon consciousness and following any ways of man, sophistication and/or intellectualism). Heavenly Father, I (we) ask You to give us deliverance and freedom from all these bondages in the Name of Christ Jesus according to John 16:23.

In the Name of the Lord Jesus Christ of Nazareth, I (we) bind all of satan's evil, wicked, demon, lying and tormenting spirits and strongmen, along with all their works, roots, fruits, tentacles and links of: partial list – (say what applies to you) – examples including: abandonment, abomination, abortion, abuse, accusation, accuser of the brethren, addictions, adultery, adulteress lust, affectation, agitation, aggravation, alcoholism, analysis, un-submissiveness, anxiety, anger, anguish, animosity, anorexia, anti-Semitism, apathy, apprehension, being argumentative, arrogance, atheism, backbiting, bad attitude, bad language, belittling, bickering, bitterness, black magic, blasphemy, blindness, burden, boasting, brainwashing, cares & riches of this world, charms, complaining, covetousness, cursing, occultism, condemnation, confusion, confrontation, conjuring, concupiscence, contention, control, conniving, plotting, criticalness, cruelty, cynicalism, daydreaming, death, deception, defeatism, deafness, dejection, delusion, depression, dependencies, despair, desires of this world, despondency, destruction, disbelief, disgust, discouragement, discontentment, disobedience, dissension, disdain, distrust, division, divination, dominance, doubt, drug abuse, drug addiction, drunkenness, dread, escapism, egoism, envy, false burdens, false compassion, false responsibility, fantasy, fantasy lust, fault finding, fear, fear of rejection, fear of man, fear of disapproval, fear of failure, fear of condemnation, fear of accusation, fear of reproof, fetishes, fighting, fatigue, forgetfulness, fornication, fortune telling, fretting, frigidity, frustrations, causing offense, gloom, gout, gossip, greed, guilt, hate, haughtiness, heaviness, hopelessness, hallucinations, harlotry, horoscopes, hurt, hyperactivity, idleness, idolatries of any kind, impurity, incest, infirmity, impatience, inadequacy, incantations, incoherence, ineptness, indecision, indifferences, insomnia, intimidation, intolerances, insecurity, insanity, irritation, jealousy, being judgmental, laboring, lasciviousness, legalism, lethargy, levitation, listlessness, loneliness, lust, lust of the eye, lust of the flesh, lust of the mind, lying, madness, mania, manipulation, masturbation, materialism, material lust, mental illness, mischief, morbidity, murder, murmuring, nervousness, nervous habits, nicotine addiction, not letting go of wickedness, oppression, paranoia, passivity, pederasty, pedophilia, pendulum, perfectionism, petulance, persecution, pornography, possessiveness, pouting, presumption, pretension, pride, procrastination, provoking, quarreling, railing, rape, rage, rebellion, rejection, restlessness, rationalization, retaliation, retardation, rigidity, resentment, rudeness, sadism, seduction, shame, slander, self-accusation, self-confusion, self-rejection, self-seduction, self-pity, selfishness, self-centeredness, self-deception, self-delusion, self-righteousness, self-condemnation, self-hatred, self-criticalness, self-willed, insensitivity, sexual idolatry, sexual impurity, shyness, sin consciousness, skepticism, sleepiness, sorrow, stiff-necked, strife, stress, stubbornness, struggling, suspicion, suicide, taking offense, tarot cards, temper, tension, tiredness, theatrics, timidity, uncleanliness, unforgiveness, undermining, unfairness, unworthiness, water witching, weariness, white magic, willful sin, withdrawal, worry, witchcraft, vanity, vindictiveness, violence, all unrighteousness, demon consciousness and following any ways of man, sophistication, intellectualism and Nimrod, high-mindedness, Jezebel, Ahab, Herodian, Python, Saul, religions, sorcery, voodoo, cults, occultism. All hindering, persecuting, accusing, lying familiar, seducing spirits, mind—binding, mind-blocking spirits, antichrist, generational spirits, all spirits and strongmen of all mental, physical, and emotional illness, sickness, diseases, disorders, death, premature death, infirmities, afflictions, inflammations, viruses, infections, abnormal cells, radical cells, lesions, cysts, pain, trauma, shock, spasms, cramps, abnormal growths, radical growths in or on any parts of our bodies including our eyes, ears, nose, mouth, throat, back, bones, muscles, ligaments, tissues, blood, blood vessels, arteries, colons, intestines, stomach, prostate, thyroid, brain, liver, heart, lungs, cardiovascular disorders and diseases, reproductive disorders and diseases, thyroid disorders and diseases, blood pressure disorders and diseases, throat disorders and diseases, breast disorders and diseases, neurological disorders and diseases, lymphatic disorders and diseases, chemical imbalances, hormone imbalances, allergies of any kind, senility, forgetfulness, paranoia, schizophrenia, all spirits of arthritis, crippling arthritis, acute arthritis, rheumatoid arthritis, sinusitis, acute sinusitis, bursitis, tendonitis, and performance spirits. All spirits of disorders and diseases, hypoglycemia of all forms, degenerative diseases of all kind, all cancers, all tumors, and all mind diseases and disorders, I (we) bind and loose all these demonic spirits and strongmen from me (us), from everyone that I (we) have prayed for today, along with all evil principalities, powers, and rulers of wickedness in high places, from every organ in our bodies, from every cell in our bodies, from every gland in our bodies, from our homes, properties, marriages, cars, trucks, businesses, ministries, objects, work places, finances . . . and I (we) loose them to go where Jesus sends them and I (we) bind them and command them to stay there in the Name of Jesus Christ of Nazareth. I (we) place the Blood of the Lord Christ Jesus between us. I (we) claim all of our lives united together in obedient love and service to the Lord Jesus Christ. Lord, I (we) ask you to grant us conviction of sin with Godly sorrow to repentance. I (we) pray that we will now be set completely free from anything that now binds us. Heavenly Father, I ask You to cause Your anointing to break and destroy every yoke of bondage in our lives. In the Name of Jesus Christ, Heavenly Father, I (we) ask you to fill our minds with the gifts of the Spirit of God, with love, joy, peace, with longsuffering, gentleness and goodness, with meekness, faithfulness and self control. Heavenly Father, in Christ Jesus' Holy Name, I (we) ask You to fill us with Your Holy Spirit anointing and power and cover us with Your presence.

Heavenly Father, I (we) bow and worship and praise before You and I (we) apply the precious Blood of the Lord Jesus Christ, from the tops of our heads to the soles of our feet. I (we) plead the Blood of Jesus over us, over the airways that surround us, over us and under us, over telephone lines, over our homes, properties, offices, cars, trucks, marriages, businesses, finances, ministries . . . I (we) plead the precious Blood of Jesus Christ and I (we) ask You to render powerless and harmless and nullify the power, destroy the power, cancel the power of any evil spirit, demonic spirit, evil strongmen, messengers of satan that try to come into our presence, our homes, our properties, our automobiles, our finances, our ministries . . . in the Name of Jesus Christ of Nazareth. Heavenly Father, in the Name of the

Lord Jesus Christ of Nazareth, I (we) thank you for Your mighty work. Grant to me the grace, power and desire to be persistent in my intercessions for ______, and myself that You may be glorified through our deliverance. In the Name of the Lord Jesus Christ of Nazareth, I (we) pray with thanksgiving. Amen!

Shattering Strongholds On Self

Heavenly Father, I come to You now in the Name of my Lord and Savior Christ Jesus. Heavenly Father, I am standing on the truth of Your Word. You said You would give me the Keys to the Kingdom, that whatsoever I would bind on earth would be bound in heaven and whatsoever I would loose on earth would be loosed in heaven according to Matthew 16 and 18. Right now, in the Name of Jesus Christ, I bind my will to the Will of God, that I will be constantly aware of Your Will and purpose for my life. I bind myself to the truth of God that I will not be deceived by the many subtle deceptions of the world and the devil. In the Name of Jesus Christ, I bind myself to the Blood of Jesus. I want to be constantly aware of the Blood of Christ Jesus' miracle working power to restore and heal and keep me safe. I bind my mind to the mind of Christ that I will be aware of how Jesus Christ would have me think and believe. I do not want to react out of my own human thoughts when situations arise suddenly. I want to think and act as Jesus would have me act. I bind my feet to paths of righteousness that my steps will be steady and true all day long. I bind myself to the work of the cross in my life so that I will continue to die daily to my own selfish desires and motivations and be more like Jesus. In the Name of Jesus Christ, I bind the strongman so that I may spoil his household and take back every bit of joy, peace, blessing, freedom and every material and spiritual possession that he has stolen from me. I take them back right now! I loose the strongman's influence over every part of my body, soul, and spirit. I loose, crush, smash and destroy every evil devise you may try to bring into my sphere of influence during this day. I repent of every wrong desire, attitude and pattern of thinking I have had. Forgive me, Heavenly Father, for holding onto wrong ideas, desires, behaviors and habits according to 1 John 1:9 and John 14:14. I renounce and reject these things in the Name of the Lord Jesus Christ, and I loose every wrong attitude, pattern of thinking, belief, idea, desire, behavior and habit I have ever learned. I loose the strongholds around them that would keep me from being completely surrendered to the will of God for my life. I loose all doubt and confusion from myself. I have bound my mind to the mind of Christ and I loose every wrong thought and evil imagination that will keep me from being in sweet unity with You. I bind and loose these things in the Name of Jesus Christ, who has given me the keys to do so. Amen!

Conclusion

This is all about having faith in God. This is a walk of faith that will take you to a new level.

Remember, if you have faith as a grain of mustard seed, nothing shall be impossible unto you, thus saith the Lord. This book is loaded with scriptures on prospering, and the key is to confess them. Open your mouth and speak; we all complain with our own mouths. So let's start speaking prosperity scriptures, God's word.

Now do not think the first time you speak this, it will happen. God is always watching you, and if you remain faithful and press on no matter what comes your way and follow this teaching, you shall prosper in all areas of your life. The main key is to practice catching up to the Third Heaven and be seated with Christ in heavenly places. Be at the right hand of Christ and speak your prayers, and your life will change.

I want to see God's people prosper and come out of financial bondage.

When you buy my book, you can write me; and I will rush to you three CDs, two on prospering God's way and a messianic praise CD that if you play these in your house, the anointing for this will be there, and breakthroughs will come in all areas of your life. This is a $30 value, and if you buy my book, it only will be only $10 for you.

You can also include your prayer requests, and this prophet will agree with you and speak good things over your life. Send a money order made out to me, John Feagin.

My address to receive this:

John Feagin
271 East Border drive
Mobile, AL. 36608
My e-mail address: pastorfeag857977@bellsouth.net
Visit my Web site: www.anointedman.com

I call you blessed!

The end.

CPSIA information can be obtained
at www.ICGtesting.com
Printed in the USA
BVHW07*1308201018
530373BV00002B/50/P

9 781441 580689